DWIGHT L. MOODY'S
DEVOTIONAL
BOOK

D.L. Moody's Devotional Book
ISBN 1-89306-505-7
Copyright © 1998 Honor Books

Published by Honor Books for Family Christian Press.
P.O. Box 55388
Tulsa, Oklahoma 74155

Compiled by James S. Bell Jr.

$\mathcal{I}$NTRODUCTION

D. L. MOODY was the foremost American evangelist of the nineteenth century, presenting the gospel in a compelling and clear manner and persuasively leading countless scores to make a decision for Christ. He preached in such a manner that the masses, at every level, could relate and comprehend. Moody was concrete, practiced, and full of common sense.

Perhaps the greatest secret of Moody's effectiveness was his gift of illustrating principles. At times his illustrations were analogies or comparisons, but more often than not, involved a full-length story that could stand on its own. Similar to the parables of Jesus, Moody's stories contained the richest lords and the impoverished beggar, life's most incredible celebrations, and its greatest tragedies.

Though many of his stories related to personal experiences or to those of close friends and family, they all represented the same human quest for God that we find today.

This dynamic collection of timeless insights, from Moody, will cause you to reach out to God with a hunger to worship and serve Him in a much fuller and deeper way.

*S*TEER *C*LEAR

A steamboat was stranded in the Mississippi River, and the captain could not get her off. Eventually a hard-looking fellow came on board, and said:

"Captain, I understand you want a pilot to take you out of this difficulty."

The captain said, "Are you a pilot?"

"Well, they call me one."

"Do you know where the snags and sandbars are?"

"No, sir."

"Well, how do you expect to take me out of here if you don't know where the snags and sandbars are?"

"I know where they ain't!" was the reply.

Beware of temptations. "Lead us not into temptation," our Lord taught us to pray; and again He said, "Watch and pray, lest ye enter into temptation." We are weak and sinful by nature, and it is a good deal better for us to pray for deliverance rather than to run into temptation and then pray for strength to resist.

◆·■··◆··■··◆··■··◆··■··◆··■··◆··■··◆··■··◆··■··◆··■··◆·

TO AVOID TEMPTATION YOU NEED TO BE
ALERT AND PRAYERFUL AT ALL TIMES.

GREEN FIELDS OR DESERT?

When I was out in California, the first time I went down from the Sierra Nevada Mountains and dropped into the Valley of the Sacramento, I was surprised to find on one farm that everything about it was green—all the trees and flowers, everything was blooming, and everything was green and beautiful, and just across the hedge everything was dried up, and there was not a green thing there. I could not understand it. I made inquiries, and I found that the man who had everything green, irrigated; he just poured the water right on, and kept everything green, while the fields that were next to his were as dry as Gideon's fleece without a drop of dew.

So it is with a great many in the church today. They are like these farms in California—a dreary desert, everything parched and desolate, and apparently no life in them. They can sit next to a man who is full of the Spirit of God, who is like a green bay tree, and who is bringing forth fruit, and yet they will not seek a similar blessing.

Well, why this difference? Because God has poured water on him who was thirsty; that is the difference.

WE BEAR FRUIT BECAUSE GOD HAS POURED WATER INTO OUR THIRSTY HEARTS.

*P*AYING *A*TTENTION TO THE *P*REACHER

*T*here was an architect in Chicago who was converted. In giving his testimony, he said he had been in the habit of attending church for a great many years, but he could not say that he had really heard a sermon all the time. He said that when the minister gave out the text and began to preach, he used to settle himself in the corner of the pew and work out the plans of some building. He could not tell how many plans he had prepared while the minister was preaching. He was the architect for one or two companies; and he used to do all his planning in that way.

You see, Satan came in between him and the preacher, and caught away the good seed of the Word. I have often preached to people, and have been perfectly amazed to find they could hardly tell one solitary word of the sermon; even the text had completely gone from them.

•─••─••─••─••─••─••─••─••─••─••─••─•

DON'T LET THE ENEMY SNATCH AWAY THE SEED OF GOD'S WORD.

ILLUMINATED CHRISTIANS

*T*here is a fable of an old lantern in a shed, which began to boast because it heard its master say he didn't know what he would ever do without it. But the little candle within spoke up and said, "Yes, you'd be a great comfort if it wasn't for me! You are nothing; I'm the one who gives the light." We are nothing, but Christ is everything, and what we want is to keep in communion with Him and let Christ dwell in us richly and shine forth through us.

I have a matchbox with a phosphorescent front. It draws in the rays of the sun during the day and then throws them out in the dead hours of the night, so that I can always see in the dark. Now, that is what we ought to be, constantly drawing in the rays of the Sun of Righteousness and then giving them out. Someone said to some young converts, "It is all moonshine, being converted." They replied, "Thank you for the compliment. The moon borrows light from the sun, and so we borrow ours from the Sun of Righteousness." That is what takes place when we have this illumination.

‹•—•—••—•—••—•—••—•—••—•—••—•—••—•—••—•—•›

THE MOON BORROWS LIGHT FROM THE SUN,
AND SO WE BORROW OURS
FROM THE SON OF RIGHTEOUSNESS.

*P*EACE *D*ECLARED

When France and England were at war, a French vessel had gone off on a long whaling voyage. When it came back, the crew was short of water, and near an English port, they wanted to get water. But they were afraid that they would be taken prisoners if they went into that port.

Some people in the port saw their signal of distress, and sent word that they need not be afraid, that the war was over, and peace had been declared. But they couldn't make those soldiers believe it, and they didn't dare to go into port, although they were out of water.

At last they made up their minds that they had better go in and surrender their cargo and their lives to their enemies rather than perish at sea without water. And when they got in, they found out that what had been told them was true, that peace had been declared.

There are a great many people who don't believe the glad tidings that peace has been made by Jesus Christ between God and man, but it is true.

WHETHER OR NOT WE BELIEVE OR
UNDERSTAND EVERYTHING ABOUT
THE GOOD NEWS, IT'S ALL STILL TRUE.

*L*ADY *P*ENDULUM

When Mr. Sankey and I were in London, a lady who attended our meetings was brought into the house in her carriage, being unable to walk. At first she was very skeptical, but one day she said to her servant:

"Take me into the inquiry room."

After I had talked with her a good while about her soul she said:

"But you will go back to America, and it will be all over."

"Oh, no," said I, "it is going to last forever."

I couldn't make her believe it. I don't know how many times I talked with her. At last I used the fable of the pendulum in the clock.

The pendulum figured up the thousands of times it would have to tick, and got discouraged, and was going to give up. Then it thought, "It is only a tick at a time," and went on. So it is in the Christian life—only one step at a time.

She began to see that if she could trust God for a supply of grace for only one day, she could go right on in the same way from day to day. As soon as she saw this, she never could get done talking about that pendulum. She had a pendulum put up in her room to remind her of the illustration, and when I went away from London she gave me a clock—I've got it in my house still.

THE CHRISTIAN LIFE MAY HAVE THOUSANDS
OF STEPS, BUT WE ONLY HAVE
TO TAKE THEM ONE AT A TIME.

HIS MINISTER'S BIBLE

If I have a right to cut out a certain portion of the Bible, I don't know why one of my friends has not a right to cut out another, and another friend to cut out another part, and so on. You would have an odd kind of Bible if everybody cut out what he wanted to! Every adulterer would cut out everything about adultery; every liar would cut out everything about lying; every drunkard would be cutting out what he didn't like.

Once a gentleman took his Bible around to his minister, and said, "This is your Bible."

"Why do you call it *my* Bible?" said the minister.

"Well," replied the gentleman, "I have been sitting under your preaching for five years, and when you said that a thing in the Bible was not authentic, I cut it out."

He had about a third of the Bible cut out; all of Job, all of Ecclesiastes and Revelation, and a good deal besides. The minister wanted him to leave the Bible with him; he didn't want the rest of his congregation to see it. But the man said:

"Oh, no! I have the covers left, and I will hold on to them."

And off he went holding on to them.

◆━◆━◆━◆━◆━◆━◆━◆━◆━◆━◆━◆━◆

IF EVERYONE HAD A RIGHT TO OMIT SOMETHING
FROM THE BIBLE WHICH OFFENDED THEM,
WE'D SOON HAVE NOTHING LEFT.

"HITCH ON" AND "CUT BEHIND"

Someone tells of an incident that happened in a New England town the other day. All the boys were sleighing. A big sleigh—we call it a "pung" up there—was being driven through the streets by an old man who looked like Santa Claus. He was calling out to the small boys to hitch on, for a pung is like a bus, it always holds one more.

There were already about twenty rollicking boys hitched on, when one little fellow dropped off behind. He tried, but couldn't catch up again, and pretty soon he began to look out for another chance for a ride. A man's sleigh was standing nearby, and the boy began to eye the man. When the man in the sleigh started off, the little fellow hitched on behind, and the man grabbed his whip and struck him directly in the eye. It looked as if the eye had been put out, but it wasn't.

Now, that's the way we go through this world. Some say, "Hitch on, hitch on"; others, "Cut behind, cut behind." The hitch-on people fill the churches, and the cut-behind ones empty them.

* * *

REACH AND ASK OTHERS
TO HITCH A RIDE TO HEAVEN.

THE BORDER APPLE TREE

I remember when I was a boy in Northfield, right near the old red schoolhouse there was an apple tree that bore the earliest apples of any tree in town.

They had a law in that town that fruit on a tree overhanging the street belonged to the public, and any fruit on the other side of the fence belonged to the property-holders. Half that apple tree was over in the street, and it got more old booms and brickbats and handles than any other tree in town. We boys used to watch to see when an apple was getting red. I never got a ripe apple from that tree in my life, and I don't believe anyone else ever did. You never went by that tree that you didn't see a lot of broomhandles and clubs up there.

Now, take a lot of Christians who want to live right on the line, with one foot in the world and one foot in the church. They get more clubs than anyone else. The world clubs them. They say, "I don't believe in that man's religion." And the church clubs them. They get clubs from both sides. It is a good deal better to keep just as far from the line as you can if you want power.

IF YOU WANT REAL PEACE AND REST IN YOUR SOUL, KEEP SEPARATED FROM THE WORLD.

Is Your Soul Insured?

"Pa," said a little boy as he climbed to his father's knee, and looked into his face as earnestly as if he understood the importance of the subject. "Pa, is your soul insured?"

"What are you thinking about, my son?" replied the agitated father. "Why do you ask that question?"

"Why, Pa, I heard Uncle George say that you had your house insured, and your life insured; but he didn't believe you had thought of your soul, and he was afraid you would lose it. Won't you get it insured right away?"

The father leaned his head on his hand, and was silent. He owned broad acres of land that were covered with a bountiful produce; his barns were even now filled with plenty, his buildings were all well covered by insurance; and as if that would not suffice for the maintenance of his wife and only child in case of his decease, he had, the day before, taken a life policy for a large amount; yet not one thought had he given to his own immortal soul. On that which was to waste away and become part and parcel of its native dust he had spared no pains; but for that which was to live on and on through the long ages of eternity he had made no provision.

"What shall it profit a man if he gain the whole world and lose his own soul?"

————————————————————

THE BEST INSURANCE AVAILABLE IS THE KIND THAT WILL KEEP YOUR SOUL FOR ETERNITY.

*W*ILLIE AND THE *B*EARS

"*I* can't take you to the park that way, Willie."

"Why, Papa? You said you would take me."

"Ah, but I can't; you're all over mud. I couldn't be seen with such a dirty little boy."

"Why, I'se clean, Papa; Mamma washed me."

"Well, you've got dirty again."

But he began to cry, and I could not convince him that he was dirty.

"I'se clean; Mamma washed me!" he cried.

Do you think I argued with him? No. I just took him up in my arms, and carried him into the house, and showed him his face in the looking glass. He had not a word to say. He would not take my word for it; but one look at the glass was enough; he saw it for himself. He didn't say he wasn't dirty after that!

Now, the looking glass showed him that his face was dirty—*but he did not take the looking glass to wash it;* of course not. The Law is the looking glass to see ourselves in, to show us our unworthiness in the sight of God; but many people take the Law and try to *wash* themselves with it, instead of being washed in the blood of the Lamb.

◆▬◆▬◆▬◆▬◆▬◆▬◆▬◆▬◆▬◆▬◆

THE LAW OF GOD WON'T WASH US CLEAN, ONLY THE BLOOD OF THE LAMB.

THE MANSION MADE READY

Once when I was traveling to a city there was a lady in the car with me. After I had reached the hotel where I was to stay, and had got comfortable quarters, she came, and said:

"Oh, sir, I cannot get a room in this hotel; they are quite full! However did you manage to get a room?"

"Easily enough," I replied. "I just telegraphed on before that I was coming, to have a room ready for me."

And it is somewhat similar in regard to gaining admission to heaven. Your names must be sent on beforehand and entered in its book, else you won't get in; but get your names inscribed on its pages, and then you won't be disappointed.

God will have a mansion ready for you when you ascend to your heavenly home. When you come to its gates, the guardian angels will refer to the book of life to see if your name is there. If so, pass in; but if not, admittance will be inexorably refused.

GOD WILL HAVE A MANSION READY FOR YOU WHEN YOU ASCEND TO YOUR HEAVENLY HOME.

Its Strength Was Underestimated

Some of the older people can remember when our Civil War broke out. Secretary Seward, who was Lincoln's Secretary of State—a long-headed and shrewd politician—prophesied that the war would be over in ninety days; and young men in thousands and hundreds of thousands came forward and volunteered to go down to Dixie and whip the South. They thought they would be back in ninety days; but the war lasted four years, and cost about half a million lives. What was the matter? Why, the South was a good deal stronger than the North supposed. Its strength was underestimated.

Jesus Christ makes no mistake of that kind. When He enlists a man in His service, He shows him the dark side; He lets him know that he must live a life of self-denial. If a man is not willing to go to heaven by the way of Calvary, he cannot go at all. Many men want a religion in which there is no cross, but they cannot enter heaven that way.

YOU CAN'T ENTER HEAVEN WITHOUT
SELF-DENIAL, SEEN BEST AT THE CROSS.

TOLLING THE BELL

I well remember how in my native village in New England it used to be customary, as a funeral procession left the church, for the bell to toll as many times as the deceased was old. How anxiously I would count those strokes of the bell to see how long I might reckon on living!

Sometimes there would be seventy or eighty tolls, and I would give a sigh of relief to think I had so many years to live. But at other times there would be only a few years tolled, and then a horror would seize me as I thought that I, too, might soon be claimed as a victim by that dread monster, Death.

Death and judgment were a constant source of fear to me till I realized the fact that neither shall ever have any hold on a child of God.

In his letter to the Romans the apostle Paul has showed, in most direct language, that there is no condemnation for a child of God, but that he is passed from under the power of law. In the Epistle to the Corinthians he tells us that "there is a natural body, and there is a spiritual body, and as we have borne the image of the earthly, we shall also bear the image of the heavenly."

WE WILL ONE DAY HAVE A SPIRITUAL BODY THAT WILL LAST FOR ETERNITY.

A Father's Neglect

A little child ran about gathering wildflowers and little blades of grass, and coming to his father and saying:

"Pretty! Pretty!"

At last the father fell asleep, and while he was sleeping the little child wandered away. When he awoke, his first thought was:

"Where is my child?"

He looked all around, but he could not see him. He shouted at the top of his voice, but all he heard was the echo. Running to a little hill, he looked around and shouted again. No response! Then going to a precipice at some distance, he looked down, and there, upon the rocks and briars, he saw the mangled form of his loved child. He rushed to the spot, took up the lifeless corpse, and hugged it to his bosom, and accused himself of being the murderer of his child. While he was sleeping his child had wandered over the precipice.

I thought as I read that, what a picture of the Church of God! How many fathers and mothers, how many Christian men and women, are sleeping now while their children wander over the terrible precipice right into the bottomless pit!

◆━◆━◆━◆━◆━◆━◆━◆━◆━◆━◆━◆━◆

DO YOU KNOW WHERE YOUR CHILDREN ARE
TONIGHT, OR ARE THEY WANDERING
ON THEIR OWN?

Not Much Up There

A friend of mine was once taken by an old man to see his riches. He took him into his grand house, showed him his beautiful pictures, his costly gold plate, his jewels, and still he said, "These are all mine. This grand hall I have built; it is called by my name; there is my insignia on it. And yet I was once a poor boy. I have made it all myself."

My friend looked at him. "Well, you've all this on earth; but what have you got up there?"

"Up where?" said the old man.

"Up in heaven."

"Well, I'm afraid I haven't got much up there."

"Ah," said my friend, "but you've got to die to leave this world; what will you take with you of all these things? You will die a beggar; for all these riches count as nothing in the kingdom of heaven. You will be a pauper; for you have no inheritance with the saints above."

The poor old man (he was poor enough in reality, though rich in all the world's goods) burst into tears. He had no hope for the future. In four months' time he was dead, and where is he now? He lived and died without God, and without hope in this world or the next.

STORE UP YOUR TREASURES FOR A MANSION IN HEAVEN.

THE GREATEST MIRACLE

*J*esus said, "The works that I do shall ye do also, and greater works than these shall ye do because I go to the Father."

I used to stumble over that. I didn't understand it. I thought what greater work could any man do than Christ had done? How could anyone raise a dead man who had been laid away in the sepulchre for days, and who had already begun to turn back to dust; how with a word could He call him forth?

But the longer I live the more I am convinced it is a greater thing to influence a man's will; a man whose will is set against God; to have that will broken and brought into subjection to God's will—or, in other words, it is a greater thing to have power over a living, sinning, God-hating man, than to quicken the dead. He who could create a world could speak a dead soul into life; but I think the greatest miracle this world has ever seen was the miracle at Pentecost. Here were men who surrounded the apostles, full of prejudice, full of malice, full of bitterness, their hands, as it were, dripping with the blood of the Son of God, and yet an unlettered man, a man whom they detested, a man whom they hated, stands up and preaches the gospel, and three thousand of them are immediately convicted and converted, and become disciples of the Lord Jesus Christ.

TO HAVE OUR STUBBORN WILLS BROKEN
BEFORE GOD IS AS POWERFUL AS
JESUS RAISING A MAN FROM THE DEAD.

*S*TOLEN *G*OODS A *B*URDEN

I heard of a boy who stole a cannonball from a navy yard. He watched his opportunity, sneaked into the yard, and secured it. But when he had it, he hardly knew what to do with it. It was heavy, and too large to conceal in his pocket, so he had to put it under his hat. When he got home with it, he dared not show it to his parents, because it would have led at once to his detection.

He said in after years it was the last thing he ever stole.

The story is told that a royal diamond valued at $600,000 was stolen from a window of a jeweler, to whom it had been given to set. A few months afterward a miserable man died a miserable death in a poor lodging house. In his pocket was found the diamond, and a letter telling how he had not dared to sell it, lest it should lead to his discovery and imprisonment. It never brought him anything but anxiety and pain.

STEALING OTHERS' GOODS ONLY BRINGS ANXIETY AND PAIN.

SMALL BEGINNINGS

An obscure man preached one Sunday to a few persons in a Methodist chapel in the South of England. A boy of fifteen years of age was in the audience, driven into the chapel by a snowstorm. The man took as his text the words, "Look unto me and be ye saved," and as he stumbled along as best he could, the light of heaven flashed into that boy's heart. He went out of the chapel saved, and soon became known as C. H. Spurgeon, the boy preacher.

The parsonage at Epworth, England, caught fire one night, and all the inmates escaped except one son. The boy came to a window, and was brought safely to the ground by two farmhands, one standing on the shoulder of the other. The boy was John Wesley. If you would realize the responsibility of that incident, if you would measure the consequences of that rescue, ask the millions of Methodists who look back to John Wesley as the founder of their denomination.

GOD RESCUES US FOR
GREAT THINGS DOWN THE ROAD.

BENDING HIS WILL

A mother told me up in Minnesota that she had a little child who took a book and threw it out of the window. She told him to go and pick it up. The little boy said, "I won't."

She said, "What?"

He said again, "I won't."

She said, "You must. Go and pick up that book."

He said he couldn't do it. She took him out, and she held him right to it. Dinnertime came and he hadn't picked up the book. She took him to dinner, and after it was over she took him out again. They sat there until teatime. When teatime came she took him in and gave him his supper, and then took him out and kept him there until bedtime. The next morning she went out again and kept him there until dinnertime. He found he was in for a life job, and he picked the book up.

She said she never had any trouble with the child afterward. Mothers, if you don't make your boy obey when he is young, he will break your heart one day.

◆━••━•━••━•━••━•━••━•━••━•━••━•◆

WE NEED OUR WILLS BENT TOWARD GOD EARLY IN LIFE.

THE PRAIRIE FIRE

Out in the Western country, in the autumn, when men go hunting and there has not been any rain for months, sometimes the prairie grass catches fire, and there comes up a very strong wind, and the flames just roll along twenty feet high, consuming man and beast. When the hunters see it coming, what do they do? They know they cannot run as fast as the fire can run. Not the fleetest horse can escape. They just take a match and light the grass around them, and let the flames sweep, and then they get into the burnt district and stand safe. They hear the flames roar as they come along, they see death coming toward them, but they do not fear, they do not tremble, because the fire has swept over the place where they are, and there is no danger. There is nothing for the fire to burn.

There is one mountain that the wrath of God has swept over—that is Mount Calvary—the fire spent its fury upon the bosom of the Son of God. Take your stand by the cross, and you will be safe for time and eternity.

THE FIRE OF GOD'S WRATH WAS SPENT AT CALVARY.

WHERE YOUR TREASURE IS

You can soon tell where a man's treasure is by his talk. If it is in heaven, he will not be long with you before he's talking about heaven; his heart is there, and so his speech isn't long in running there, too. If his heart is in money, he will soon have you deep in talk about mines, speculation, stocks, bank rates, and so on. If his heart is in lands, it won't be long before he's talking about real estate, improvements, houses, and so on. Always the same, wherever a man's heart is, there his tongue will be sure to go.

Someone in England said, if you see a man's goods and furniture come down by the luggage train, you're pretty sure he'll be down by the next passenger train; he won't be long after; he'll follow his goods. And so it is with heaven; if your treasure is on before you, you'll be wanting to follow it; you'll be glad to be on the road thither as soon as possible.

◆••◆••◆••◆••◆••◆••◆••◆••◆••◆••◆

IT'S NOT LONG BEFORE YOU TALK ABOUT
THE THINGS THAT MOST INTEREST YOU.

CONVERTED THE REGULAR WAY

One night, as I was preaching on the bank of a river, I happened to take for my text the words of Namaan: "I thought; I thought." I was trying to take men's thoughts up and to show the difference between their thoughts and God's thoughts. This man happened to be walking along the bank of the river. He saw a great crowd and heard someone talking, and he wondered to himself what that man was talking about. He didn't know who was there, so he drew up to the crowd and listened. He heard the sermon, and became convicted and converted right there. Then he inquired who was the preacher, and he found out it was the very man that he said he would not hear—the man he disliked. The very man he had been talking against was the very man God used to convert him.

SOMETIMES GOD USES THE VERY THINGS
WE RESIST TO BRING US TO HIM.

*H*ONEY *D*EW

I have sometimes been in a place where the very air seemed to be charged with the breath of God, like the moisture in the air. I remember one time as I went through the woods near Mount Hermon school I heard bees, and asked what it meant.

"Oh," said one of the men, "they are after the *honey dew.*"

"What is that?" I asked.

He took a chestnut leaf and told me to put my tongue to it. I did so, and the taste was sweet as honey. Upon inquiry I found that all up and down the Connecticut valley what they call "honey dew" had fallen, so that there must have been altogether hundreds of tons of honey dew in this region. Where it comes from I don't know.

Do you suppose that this earth would be worth living on if it were not for the dew and the rain? So a church that hasn't any of the dew of heaven, any of the rain that comes down in showers, will be as barren as the earth would be without the dew and rain.

WE NEED THE DEW OF HEAVEN FROM THE HOLY SPIRIT TO FALL UPON OUR CHURCHES.

CLIMB HIGHER

A friend had described how he had been up a mountain to spend the night and see the sun rise. As the party was climbing up the mountain, and before they had reached the summit, a storm came on. This friend said to the guide:

"I will give this up; take me back."

The guide smiled, and replied, "I think we shall get above the storm soon."

On they went, and it was not long before they got up to where it was as calm as any summer evening. Down in the valley a terrible storm raged; they could hear the thunder rolling, and see the lightning's flash; but all was serene on the mountaintop.

"And so, my young friends," continued the friend, "though all is dark around you, come a little higher, and the darkness will flee away."

Often when I have been inclined to get discouraged, I have thought of what he said. If you are down in the valley amidst the thick fog and the darkness, get a little higher. Get nearer to Christ, and know more of Him.

THOUGH WE FACE THE STORMS OF LIFE, AS WE CLIMB HIGHER, GOD WILL MAKE THINGS CLEAR.

"Too Late!"

At our church in Chicago I was closing the meeting one day, when a young soldier got up and entreated the people to decide for Christ at once. He said he had just come from a dark scene.

A comrade of his, who had enlisted with him, had a father who was always entreating him to become a Christian, and in reply he always said he would when the war was over. At last he was wounded, and was put into the hospital, but got worse, and was gradually sinking. One day, a few hours before he died, a letter came from his sister, but he was too far gone to read it. It was such an earnest letter! The comrade read it to him, but he did not seem to understand it, he was so weak, till it came to the last sentence, which said:

"Oh, my dear brother, when you get this letter, will you not accept your sister's Savior?"

The dying man sprang up from his cot, and said, "What do you say? What do you say?" And then, falling back on his pillow, feebly exclaimed, *"It is too late! It is too late!"*

My dear friends, thank God it is not *too late* for you today.

IT IS NOT TOO LATE TO TURN TO GOD NO MATTER WHAT YOUR CONDITION.

A Brighter Picture

Some years ago I heard of a poor woman who sent her boy to school and college. When he was to graduate, he wrote his mother to come, but she sent back word that she could not because her best skirt had already been turned once.

She was so shabby that she was afraid he would be ashamed of her. He wrote back that he didn't care how she was dressed, and urged so strongly that she went.

He met her at the station, and took her to a nice place to stay. The day came for his graduation, and he walked down the broad aisle with that poor mother dressed very shabbily, and put her into one of the best seats in the house. To her great surprise he was the valedictorian of the class, and he carried everything before him. He won a prize, and when it was given to him, he stepped down before the whole audience and kissed his mother, and said:

"Here, Mother, here is the prize! It's yours. I would not have won it if it had not been for you."

Thank God for such a man!

GIVE CREDIT TO WHOM CREDIT IS DUE,
FOR WE DO NOT ACHIEVE GREAT THINGS
WITHOUT THE HELP OF OTHERS.

It Seemed Too Good to be True

Some time ago I read in one of the daily papers a thing that pleased me very much. When the new administration of President McKinley went into office some clerks in one of the departments were promoted. One young lady was offered a promotion, but she went to see the secretary, General Butterworth, and said that there was a girl sitting next to her who had a family to support. A brother who had been supporting the family had died, or sickened, and it had fallen upon her, and she asked the general to let her friend who sat next to her have the promotion in her place.

The general said that he had heard of such things in other generations, but he didn't know that it would ever happen in his generation. He was amazed to find a person on duty in Washington who was willing to give up her position and take a lower one, and let someone else have it that she might be able to help her family. I know of nothing that speaks louder for Christ and Christianity than to see a man or woman giving up what they call their rights for others, and "in honor preferring one another."

GIVE UP YOUR RIGHTS FOR THE GOOD OF OTHERS EVEN IF IT MEANS PERSONAL SUFFERING.

CALLING A MAN A LIAR

A great many men say, "Oh, I have profound reverence and respect for God."

Yes, profound respect, but not faith. Why, it is a downright insult!

Suppose a man says, "Mr. Moody, I have profound respect for you, profound admiration for you, but I do not believe a word you say."

I wouldn't give much for his respect or admiration; I wouldn't give much for his friendship. God wants us to put our faith in Him.

How it would wound a mother's feelings to hear her children say, "I do love Mamma so much, but I don't believe what she says." How it would grieve that mother.

And that is about the way a great many of God's professed children talk. Some men seem to think it is a great misfortune that they do not have faith. Bear in mind it is not a misfortune, but it is the damning sin of the world.

RESPECT AND FRIENDSHIP DO NOT EQUAL TOTAL FAITH IN SOMEONE.

THERE MUST BE ROOTS

Suppose I hire two men to set out trees, and after a day or two I go out to see how they are getting along. I find that one man has set out a hundred trees, and the other only ten. I say:

"Look here, what does this mean? That man has set out a hundred trees, and you have set out only ten. What does it mean?"

"Yes, but he has cut off all the roots, and just stuck the tops into the ground."

I go to the other man, and say, "What does this mean? Why have you planted all of these trees without roots?"

"I don't believe in roots, they are of no account. My trees look just as well as his."

But when the sun blazes upon the trees, they all wither and die.

There are a lot of people running around who haven't got any roots. A good many live on negations. They are always telling me what they *don't* believe. I want a man to tell me what he *does* believe, not what he does not believe.

●◆••◆••◆•◆••◆••◆•◆••◆•◆••◆••◆•◆••◆••◆•

OUR ROOT AND FOUNDATION MUST BE
IN THE STRONG BELIEF IN JESUS CHRIST
AND WHAT HE HAS DONE FOR US.

It Takes Time

*S*uppose I should send my little boy, five years old, to school tomorrow morning, and when he comes home in the afternoon, say to him:

"Willie, can you read? Can you write? Can you spell? Do you understand all about algebra, geometry, Hebrew, Latin, and Greek?"

"Why, Papa," the little fellow would say, "how funny you talk. I have been all day trying to learn the A, B, C's!"

Suppose I should reply, "If you have not finished your education, you need not go anymore." What would you say? Why, you would say I had gone mad!

There would be just as much reason in that, as in the way that people talk about the Bible. The men who have studied the Bible for fifty years have never gotten down to the depths of it yet. There are truths there that the Church of God has been searching out for the last nineteen hundred years, but no man has yet fathomed the depths of the ever-living stream.

It takes time to fathom the depths of God's truth.

THE FIRST "DON'T WORRY CLUB"

Mrs. Sangster says that we hear a good deal in this age, as if it were a novelty, about the futility of being anxious, and people have established "Don't Worry Clubs." But the first "Don't Worry Club" was begun by our blessed Lord Himself when He said, "Take no thought for the morrow, for the morrow shall take thought for the things of itself. Sufficient unto the day is the evil thereof."

He bade us consider the lilies growing in their beauty and purity without a thought, and taught us the true way of living without care, without solicitude, bearing all burdens lightly, and having continual joy on our faces. Only those who have the indwelling Christ in their hearts can walk through this world with bright and glad looks, because they know that, let come what may, their Father is leading them safely.

WITH CHRIST IN OUR HEARTS
WE NEVER NEED TO WORRY.

HOW THE MINERS WERE SAVED

*I*n the north of England they have been digging the coal for a century. They have gone miles and miles away from the shaft, under the sea, and there is danger of men getting lost. I heard of two old miners who lost their way. Their lights went out, and they were in danger of losing their lives. After wandering around for a long time, they sat down and one of them said:

"Let us sit perfectly quiet, and see if we cannot feel which way the air is moving, because it always moves toward the shaft."

There they sat for a long time, when all at once one of them felt a slight touch on his cheek, and he sprang to his feet and said:

"I felt it!"

They went in the direction in which the air was moving, and reached the shaft.

Sometimes there comes a little breath from God that touches our souls. It may be so gentle and faint that you barely recognize it; but if you do, do not disregard it. Thank God that He has spoken to you, praise Him for it, and whatever may come do not go in the opposite direction.

OPEN YOUR HEART TO THE GENTLE BREEZE OF GOD'S SPIRIT.

ETERNAL VALUES

An old minister in Kentucky had a son in Chicago in the real estate business, and with the son it was "real estate, real estate," morning, noon, and night. The old father came to visit him, and he found his boy's mind full of real estate. He had lost all his Christianity. He could talk of nothing but corner lots, corner lots, corner lots. He seemed to live on corner lots. The old gentleman was very much grieved. One day he went down to the office and his son said, "Father, I am going out for a few minutes, and if anyone comes in, you can tell them there is a very good lot here that is worth so much; and here is another nice lot that is worth so much; and here is a good one that is worth so much" and so on.

The old gentleman didn't have much heart for the business; his thoughts were elsewhere. By and by a gentleman came in to inquire about a lot, and the old minister said, "My son says this lot is worth so much. And here's another one worth so much. I don't know anything about them, but I tell you, my friend, I would give more for standing room in the New Jerusalem than for all the corner lots in Chicago." And the son came in and found that his father had gone to preaching. You can tell where the heart is by what it is set upon. It is a good thing to be sure of standing room in the New Jerusalem.

WHERE YOUR TREASURE IS, THERE YOUR HEART WILL BE ALSO.

*R*EACHING THE *U*NCHURCHED

*T*here was a man who came to Christ in Chicago who couldn't speak a word of English. We had to make use of an interpreter, and what to do with that man after he became a Christian I didn't know. He wanted to do something for the Lord, and finally, I stationed him at the corner of Clark and Madison streets to give out handbills inviting people to hear me preach at the YMCA hall. And when the Lord converted him the man was so happy! His face was just lit up, and to every person who went by — and there were some pretty hard cases — he gave a handbill. And some thanked him and some swore at him, but he kept smiling all the time. He couldn't tell the difference between thanks and curses.

For two months he stood there, without a hat part of the time, and every night he was there. When it got to be dark in the short days, he would have a lantern all lit up right there on the corner. There he stood for months and months, and the Lord gave him a good many souls. What could you do if you would only try?

TEACH US, LORD, HOW TO USE YOUR TOWEL
AND WASH ONE ANOTHER'S FEET.

REAPING MORE THAN YOU SOW

*I*f I sow a bushel, I expect to reap ten or twenty bushels. The Spaniards have this proverb, "Sow a thought and reap an act. Sow an act and reap a habit. Sow a habit and reap a character. Sow a character and reap a destiny." I have heard of a certain kind of bean that reproduces itself a thousandfold. One thistledown which blew from the deck of a vessel is said to have covered with thistles the entire surface of a South Sea island. The oak springs from an acorn, the mighty Mississippi from a little spring.

One glass of whisky may lead to a drunkard's death. One lie may ruin a man's career. One error in youth may follow a man all through life. Someone has said that many a Christian spends half his time trying to keep down the sprouts of seeds sown in his young days. Unless it is held in check, the desire to "have a drink" will become a consuming thirst; the desire to "play a game of cards" an insatiable gambler's passion.

YOU REAP WHAT YOU SOW.

DON'T SWEAR!

I was greatly amazed not long ago, in talking to a man who thought he was a Christian, to find that once in awhile, when he got angry, he would swear. I said, "My friend, I don't see how you can tear down with one hand what you are trying to build up with the other. I don't see how you can profess to be a child of God and let those words come out of your lips."

He replied, "Mr. Moody, if you knew me, you would understand. I have a very quick temper. I inherited it from my father and mother, and it is uncontrollable; but my swearing comes only from the lips."

When God said, "I will not hold him guiltless that takes My name in vain," He meant what He said, and I don't believe anyone can be a true child of God who takes the name of God in vain.

* * *

I DON'T BELIEVE ANYONE CAN BE A TRUE CHILD OF GOD WHO TAKES THE NAME OF GOD IN VAIN.

*L*OVE IS THE *N*ATURE OF *G*OD

*O*ne night a man was going by and he saw the gas-lighted text, "GOD IS LOVE," and he said to himself, "God is love, God is love." By and by he came back, and he looked at it again. I saw him come in and take a seat by the door. Soon he put his hands up to his face, and once in a while I would see tears running down his cheeks, and I was foolish enough to think they were caused by my preaching.

I went to him and said, "What is the trouble?"

"I don't know."

"What was there in the sermon that made you cry?"

"I didn't know you had been preaching."

"Well, what was it that troubled you; was it anything in the songs?"

"I don't know anything about the songs."

"Well," I said, "what is the matter?"

"That text up there," he replied.

"My man," I said, "do you believe that God loves you?"

"I am not worth loving."

"That's true," I said, "but He loves you all the more." And I sat there a half hour, and the truth of God's love shone into his soul and he became a new man.

THE OVERWHELMING LOVE OF GOD TO EACH OF US SINNERS CAUSES US TO WEEP WITH JOY.

THE WRONG PHYSICIAN

I heard once of a man who went to England from the Continent, and brought letters with him to eminent physicians from the Emperor. The letters said:

"This man is a personal friend of mine, and we are afraid he is going to lose his reason. Do all you can for him."

The doctor asked him if he had lost any dear friend in his own country, or any position of importance, or what it was that was weighing on his mind. The young man said, "No, but my father and grandfather and I were brought up infidels, and for the last two or three years this thought has been haunting me, 'Where shall I spend eternity?' And the thought of it follows me day and night."

The doctor said, "You have come to the wrong physician, but I will tell you of One Who can cure you." And he told him of Christ, and read to him the fifty-third chapter of Isaiah, "With His stripes we are healed."

The young man said, "Doctor, do you believe that?"

The doctor told him he did, and prayed and wrestled with him, and at last the clear light of Calvary shone on his soul. He had settled the question in his own mind at last, where he would spend eternity.

SETTLE IN YOUR MIND THE QUESTION
AS TO WHERE YOU WILL SPEND ETERNITY.

WHAT SEED ARE YOU SOWING?

Suppose I meet a man who is sowing seed, and say, "Hello, stranger, what are you sowing?"

"Seed."

"What kind of seed?"

"I don't know."

"Don't you know whether it is good or bad?"

"No, I can't tell. But it is seed—that is all I want to know, and I am sowing it."

You would say that he was a first-class lunatic, wouldn't you? But he wouldn't be half so mad as the man who goes on sowing for time and eternity, and never asks himself what he is sowing or what the harvest will be.

Father, what seed are you sowing in your family? Are you setting your children a good or bad example? Do you spend your time at the saloon or the club, until you have become almost a stranger to them? Or are you training them for God and righteousness?

◆◆◆◆◆◆◆◆◆◆◆◆◆◆◆◆◆◆

WHAT SEEDS ARE YOU SOWING IN EVERY AREA OF YOUR LIFE, AND WHAT FRUIT WILL IT BEAR FOR ETERNITY?

Why His Life was Spared

A Confederate soldier was on sentry duty on the edge of a wood. It was a dark night and very cold, and he was a little frightened because the enemy was supposed to be near at hand. He felt very homesick and miserable, and about midnight, when everything was very still, he was beginning to feel very weary and thought that he would comfort himself by praying and singing a hymn. He remembered singing this hymn—

> 'All my trust on Thee is stayed,
>   All my help from Thee I bring,
> Cover my defenseless head
>   With the shadow of Thy wing.'

After he had sung those words a strange peace came down upon him, and through the long night he remembered having felt no more fear.

"Now," said another man, "listen to my story. I was a Union soldier, and was in the wood that night with a party of scouts. I saw you standing up, although I didn't see your face, and my men had their rifles focused upon you waiting the word to fire, but when you sang out—

> 'Cover my defenseless head
>
> With the shadow of Thy wing.'

I said, 'Boys, put down your rifles; we will go home.' I couldn't kill you after that."

━━━━━━━━━━━━━━━━━━━

TRUST IN GOD TO BE YOUR DEFENSE, EVEN IN THE MOST DANGEROUS CIRCUMSTANCES.

THE USUAL WAY

At one time I used to read so many chapters of the Bible a day, and if I did not get through my usual quantity, I thought I was getting cold and backsliding. But, mind you, if a man had asked me two hours afterward what I had read, I could not tell him; I had forgotten it nearly all.

When I was a boy I used to, among other things, hoe corn on a farm; and I used to hoe it so badly, in order to get over so much ground, that at night I had to put down a stick in the ground, so as to know next morning where I had left off.

That was somewhat in the same fashion as running through so many chapters every day. A man will say, "Wife, did I read that chapter?"

"Well," says she, "I don't remember."

And neither of them can recollect. And perhaps he reads the same chapter over and over again; and they call that "studying the Bible." I do not think there is a book in the world we neglect so much as the Bible.

STUDY THE BIBLE DILIGENTLY RATHER THAN JUST READING IT.

LOOKING FOR REVIVALS

Men are anxious for a revival in business. There is a great revival in politics just now. In all departments of life you find that men are very anxious for a revival in the things that concern them most.

If this is legitimate—and it is perfectly right in its place—should not every child of God be praying for and desiring a revival of godliness in the world at the present time? Do we not need a revival of downright honesty, of truthfulness, of uprightness, and of temperance? Are there not many who have become alienated from the Church of God and from the house of the Lord, who are forming an attachment to the saloon? Are not our sons being drawn away by the hundreds and thousands, so that while you often find the churches empty, the liquor shops are crowded every Sabbath afternoon and evening? I am sure the saloon keepers are glad if they can have a revival in their business; they do not object to selling more whisky and beer. Then surely every true Christian ought to desire that men who are in danger of perishing eternally should be saved and rescued.

SEEK FOR A REVIVAL IN YOUR SPIRITUAL LIFE, OVER YOUR BUSINESS OR OTHER PERSONAL CONCERNS.

"*That's Me!*"

While we were in London, Mr. Spurgeon one day in his orphanage told about the boys—that some of them had aunts and some cousins, and that nearly every boy had some friend who took an interest in him, and came to see him and gave him a little pocket money. One day, he said, while he stood there, a little boy came up to him and said:

"Mr. Spurgeon, let me speak to you."

The boy sat down between Mr. Spurgeon and the elder who was with him, and said:

"Mr. Spurgeon, suppose your father and mother were dead, and you didn't have any cousins, or aunts, or uncles or friends to come and give you pocket money, and give you presents, don't you think you would feel bad? Because that's me!"

Said Mr. Spurgeon, "The minute he said that, I put my right hand down into my pocket and took out some money for him."

BE GENEROUS BECAUSE YOU NEVER KNOW HOW NEEDY OTHERS REALLY ARE.

Your Own Picture There

The Bible is like an album. I go into a man's house, and while waiting for him, I take up an album and open it. I look at a picture. "Why, that looks like a man I know." I turn over and look at another. "Well, I know that man." I keep turning over the leaves. "Well, there is a man who lives in the same street as myself—he is my next-door neighbor." And then I come upon another, and see myself.

My friends, if you read your Bibles you will find your own picture there. It just describes you. You may be a Pharisee; if so, turn to the third chapter of John, and see what Christ said to the Pharisees: "Except a man be born again he cannot enter the kingdom of God." But you may say: "I am not a Pharisee; I am a poor miserable sinner, too bad to come to Him." Well, turn to the woman of Samaria, and see what Christ said to her.

IT IS IN THE BIBLE THAT YOU WILL SEE THE CLEAREST PICTURE OF YOURSELF.

A Hundred Years Hence

Once, as I was walking down the street, I heard some people laughing and talking aloud. One of them said:

"Well, there will be no difference; it will be all the same a hundred years hence."

The thought flashed across my mind, "Will there be no difference? Where will you be a hundred years hence?"

Just ask yourself the question, "Where shall I be?" Some of you who are getting on in years may be in eternity ten years hence. Where will you be, on the left or the right hand of God? I cannot tell your feelings, but I can my own. I ask you, "Where will you spend eternity? Where will you be a hundred years hence?"

ONE HUNDRED YEARS FROM NOW YOU'LL BE
EITHER AT GOD'S RIGHT HAND
OR YOU'LL DEPART FROM HIM FOREVER.

"HE IS MY BROTHER!"

A fearful storm was raging, when the cry was heard: "Man overboard!"

A human form was seen manfully breasting the furious elements in the direction of the shore; but the raging waves bore the struggler rapidly outward, and ere the boats could be lowered, a fearful space separated the victim from help. Above the shriek of the storm and roar of the waters rose his rending cry. It was an agonizing moment. With bated breath and blanched cheek, every eye was strained to the struggling man. Manfully did the brave rowers strain every nerve in that race of mercy, but all their efforts were in vain. One wild shriek of despair, and the victim went down. A piercing cry, "Save him, save him!" rang through the hushed crowd; and into their midst darted an agitated man, throwing his arms wildly in the air, shouting, "A thousand pounds for the man who saves his life!" but his staring eyes rested only on the spot where the waves rolled remorselessly over the perished. He whose strong cry broke the stillness of the crowd was the captain of the ship from whence the drowned man fell. He was *his brother.*

This is the feeling we should have in the various ranks of those bearing commission under the great Captain of our salvation. "Save him! He is my brother."

-------◆--------

LET US LOOK UPON THOSE WHO ARE PERISHING AS IF THEY WERE OUR OWN BROTHERS AND SISTERS CRYING FOR HELP.

THEIR PRAYERS ANSWERED

I remember when preaching on one occasion to an immense audience in the Agricultural Hall in London, a father and mother were in great distress about their absent son, who had given up God's ways and had wandered from his father's home to the wild bush of Australia. These poor parents asked the united prayers of that vast congregation for their son, and I suppose fully 20,000 rose to the mercy seat. It was ascertained afterward that at the very hour those prayers ascended from the audience in London, that young man was riding through the Australian bush to a town a day's ride from his camp. Something had caused him to think of his home and his parents, and as he sat in the saddle, the Spirit of God descended upon him, and he was convicted of sin. Dismounting, he knelt down by his horse's side and prayed to God for forgiveness, and in a little while he was assured of conversion. When he reached the town, he wrote the good news to his delighted mother, and asked if they would receive him at home. The answer flashed along the cable beneath the ocean:

"Come home at once."

So afraid were they that he might arrive in the night when they were not awake to receive him, that they fastened a big bell to the door, so that all the family would be awakened as he entered.

THERE IS GREAT POWER IN UNITED, CORPORATE PRAYER.

An Awful Awakening

*I*n a town of Switzerland a few years ago, some working men going early to work, walking along the street, saw a white figure on the top of a high house. What was it? A lady in her nightdress; and she was sitting looking down, quite happy, smiling in perfect security. She was a somnambulist. She had risen in her sleep without anyone in the house knowing it, and had taken her station, and was pleasantly looking about, and no doubt dreaming— dreaming pleasant dreams.

They didn't know what they could do to save her from her peril. Just as they were talking together, the sun rose. A bright beam fell upon her eyes. As she awakened and saw where she was, she gazed one moment around, and then fell headlong—killed on the spot. It was an awful awakening!

Fellow sinner, if you are out of Christ, and the day of His coming overtakes you—oh, what if the first beam of that bright day be the first moment of your awakening, and it is too late!

DON'T WALK IN THIS WORLD AS IF ASLEEP
AND NOT AWARE OF YOUR PERIL;
TURN TO THE LIGHT OF CHRIST.

ARE YOU SEEKING REST?

A lady in Wales told me this little story: An English friend of hers, a mother, had a child who was sick. At first they considered there was no danger, until one day the doctor came in and said that the symptoms were very unfavorable. He took the mother out of the room, and told her that the child could not live. It came like a thunderbolt. After the doctor had gone the mother went into the room where the child lay and began to talk to the child, and tried to divert its mind.

"Darling, do you know you will soon hear the music of heaven? You will hear a sweeter song than you have ever heard on earth. You will hear them sing the song of Moses and the Lamb. You are very fond of music. Won't it be sweet, darling?"

And the little, tired, sick child turned its head away, and said, "Oh, Mamma, I am so tired and so sick that I think it would make me worse to hear all that music."

"Well," the mother said, "you will soon see Jesus. You will see the seraphim and cherubim and the streets all paved with gold."

Dear friend, are you not tired and weary of sin? Are you not weary of the turmoil of life? You can find rest on the bosom of the Son of God.

IF YOU ARE WEARY YOU CAN FIND REST IN JESUS.

A New Man
IN Old Clothes

A man got up in one of our meetings in New York some years ago who had been pretty far down, but a wonderful change had taken place, and he said he hardly knew himself. He said the fact was, he was a new man in his old clothes.

That was just it. Not a man in new clothes, but a new man in old clothes.

I saw an advertisement which read like this: "If you want people to respect you, wear good clothes." That is the world's idea of getting the world's respect. Why, a leper may put on good clothes, but he is a leper still. Mere profession doesn't transform a man. It is the new nature spoken of in 2 Corinthians, the fifth chapter, and the 17th verse, "Therefore if any man be in Christ, he is a new creature; old things are passed away; behold, all things are become new."

PUT ON THE GARMENTS OF SALVATION,
BECAUSE THE OLD CREATURE CANNOT BE
TRANSFORMED BY EARTHLY CLOTHES.

WHAT COULD THE KING DO?

*I*n the second century they brought a Christian before a king, who wanted him to recant and give up Christ and Christianity, but the man spurned the proposition.

But the king said, "If you don't do it, I will banish you."

The man smiled and answered, "You can't banish me from Christ, for He says He will never leave me nor forsake me."

The king got angry, and said, "Well, I will confiscate your property and take it all from you."

And the man replied, "My treasures are laid up on high; you cannot get them."

The king became still more angry, and said, "I will kill you."

"Why," the man answered, "I have been dead forty years; I have been dead with Christ, dead to the world, and my life is hid with Christ in God, and you cannot touch it."

"What are you going to do with such a fanatic?" said the king.

* • •• • • •• • • •• • • •• • • •• • • •• • • •• • • •• • •

WE CANNOT REALLY LOSE ANYTHING
WHEN PERSECUTED BECAUSE WE HAVE
ALREADY DIED TO IT ALL IN CHRIST.

THE POWER IN PREACHING

*H*arry Morehouse, the English Bible preacher, said to me when visiting the church I pastored in Chicago, "If you will stop preaching your own words and preach God's Word, He will make you a great power for good." This prophecy made a deep impression on me, and from that time I devoted myself to the study of the Bible as I had never done before. I had been accustomed to draw my sermons from the experiences of Christians and the life of the streets, but now I began to follow the counsel of my friend and preach the Word.

My first series of sermons on characters in the Bible was preached the summer before the great Chicago fire, and I was surprised by the attention these teachings received. I also began to compare scripture with scripture. "If I don't understand a text," I said to my friend Morehouse, "I ask another text to explain it, and then if it is too hard for me, I take it to the Lord and ask Him about it." I have learned that the best source for sermons that help people is the Bible.

THE WORD OF GOD IS SHARPER
THAN ANY TWO-EDGED SWORD.

"MIND YOUR OWN BUSINESS!"

One night in Chicago, many years ago, when I was on my way home I saw a man leaning against a lamppost. Stepping up to him and placing my hand on his shoulder, I said, "Are you a Christian?"

The man flew into a rage, doubled up his fist, and I thought he was going to pitch me into the gutter.

I said, "I'm very sorry if I've offended you, but I thought I was asking a proper question."

"Mind your own business," he roared.

"That is my business," I answered.

About three months later, on a bitter cold morning about daybreak, someone knocked at my door.

"Who's there?" I asked.

A stranger answered, and I said, "What do you want?"

"I want to become a Christian," was the reply.

I opened the door, and to my astonishment there was the man who had cursed me for talking to him as he leaned against the lamppost.

He said, "I'm very sorry. I haven't had any peace since that night. Your words have haunted and troubled me. I couldn't sleep last night, and I thought I'd come and get you to pray for me."

⋅•⋅••⋅•⋅••⋅•⋅••⋅•⋅••⋅•⋅••⋅•⋅••⋅•⋅•

OUR BUSINESS IS MERELY TO SHARE THE GOSPEL, AND GOD WILL DO THE REST.

THANK GOD FOR THE RESURRECTION!

At the battle of Inkerman a soldier was just able to crawl to his tent after he was struck down. When found, he was lying upon his face, his open Bible before him, his hand glued fast to the page by his life blood which covered it. Then his hand was lifted, the letters of the printed page were clearly traced upon it, and with the ever-living promise in and on his hand, they laid him in a soldier's grave. The words were:

"I am the resurrection and the life; he that believeth in Me, though he were dead, yet shall he live."

I want a religion that can comfort even in death, that can unite me with my loved ones. Oh, what gloom and darkness would settle upon this world if it was not for the glorious doctrine of the resurrection! Thank God, the glorious morning will soon break. For a little while God asks us to be on the watchtower, faithful to Him and waiting for the summons. Soon our Lord will come to receive His own, whether they be living or dead.

THE RESURRECTION IS A PAST REALITY AND A WONDERFUL FUTURE HOPE.

OUT OF THE POORHOUSE

A few years ago, I was going away to preach one Sunday morning, when a young man drove up in front of us. He had an aged woman with him.

"Who is that young man?" I asked.

"Do you see that beautiful meadow?" said my friend, "and that land there with the house upon it?"

"Yes."

"His father drank that all up," said he; and he went on to tell me all about him. His father was a great drunkard, squandered his property, died and left his wife in the poorhouse. "And that young man is one of the finest young men I ever knew. He has toiled hard and earned money, and bought back the land; he has taken his mother out of the poorhouse, and now he is taking her to church."

I thought, that is an illustration for me. The first Adam in Eden sold us for naught, but the Messiah, the second Adam, came and bought us back again. The first Adam brought us to the poorhouse, as it were; the second Adam makes us kings and priests unto God. That is redemption. We get in Christ all that Adam lost, and more. Men look on the blood of Christ with scorn and contempt, but the time is coming when the blood of Christ will be worth more than all the kingdoms of the world.

--------◆--◆--◆--◆--◆--◆--◆--◆--◆--◆--◆--------

CHRIST BOUGHT BACK BY HIS BLOOD ALL THAT WE LOST AND MAKES US KINGS AND PRIESTS.

ANOTHER KIND OF PARDON

During the war a boy in Pennsylvania was condemned to death. The boy expected to be pardoned and was resting upon that hope. The papers were full of statements that Governor Curtin would pardon the boy. One day Governor Curtin met Mr. George H. Stuart, the noted philanthropist, on the street, and said:

"Stuart, you know this boy who is sentenced to death. He is entertaining a hope that I am going to pardon him, and I can't do it. Now, go and tell him."

Mr. Stuart afterward told me that it was the hardest duty he had ever performed, but it was an act of mercy. When he entered the cell the prisoner rushed to him and cried:

"Mr. Stuart, you are a good man; I know you bring me a pardon."

Mr. Stuart knew not what to answer, but he summoned the courage and told the boy the truth. The boy fell in a faint at Mr. Stuart's feet when he found his false hope taken away, but it prepared the way to tell him where alone a true and lasting hope might be found.

TRUE AND LASTING FORGIVENESS COMES ONLY FROM GOD.

THEY ARE OLD ENOUGH

I have no sympathy with the idea that our children have to grow up before they are converted. Once I saw a lady with three daughters at her side, and I stepped up to her and asked her if she was a Christian.

"Yes, sir."

Then I asked the oldest daughter if she was a Christian. The chin began to quiver, and the tears came into her eyes, and she said:

"I wish I was."

The mother looked very angrily at me and said, "I don't want you to speak to my children on that subject. They don't understand." And in great rage she took them all away from me. One daughter was fourteen years old, one twelve, and the other ten, but they were not old enough to be talked to about religion! Let them drift into the world and plunge into worldly amusements, and then see how hard it is to reach them. Many a mother is mourning today because her boy has gone beyond her reach, and will not allow her to pray with him. She may pray *for* him, but he will not let her pray or talk *with* him. In those early days when his mind was tender and young, she might have led him to Christ. Bring them in. "Suffer the little children to come unto Me."

◆•••◆••◆••◆•◆••◆•◆••◆••◆•◆••◆••◆•

GOD ALLOWS EVEN LITTLE CHILDREN TO UNDERSTAND THE GOOD NEWS.

*S*PURGEON'S *P*ARABLE

*M*r. Spurgeon once made a parable. He said, "There was once a tyrant who summoned one of his subjects into his presence, and ordered him to make a chain. The poor blacksmith—that was his occupation—had to go work and forge the chain. When it was done, he brought it into the presence of the tyrant, and was ordered to take it away and make it twice the length. He brought it again to the tyrant, and again he was ordered to double it. Back he came when he had obeyed the order, and the tyrant looked at it, and then commanded the servants to bind the man hand and foot with the chain he had made and cast him into prison.

"That is what the devil does with men," Mr. Spurgeon said. "He makes them forge their own chain, and then binds them hand and foot with it, and casts them into outer darkness."

* * *

THE DEVIL HELPS US TO CREATE OUR BONDAGE WHEN WE FALL INTO SIN.

A Beautiful Legend

There is a beautiful tradition connected with the site on which the temple of Solomon was erected. It is said to have been occupied in common by two brothers, one of whom had a family, the other did not. On this spot was sown a field of wheat. On the evening succeeding the harvest—the wheat having been gathered in separate shocks—the elder brother said to his wife:

"My younger brother is unable to bear the burden and heat of the day; I will arise, take of my shocks and place with his without his knowledge."

The younger brother being actuated by the same benevolent motives, said within himself:

"My elder brother has a family, and I have none. I will arise, take of my shocks, and place them with his."

Judge of their mutual astonishment, when, on the following day, they found their respective shocks undiminished. This transpired for several nights, when each resolved in his own mind to stand guard and solve the mystery. They did so, and on the following night they met each other halfway between their respective shocks with their arms full. Upon ground hallowed by such associations as this was the temple of Solomon erected—so spacious and magnificent—the wonder and admiration of the world! Alas! In these days, how many would sooner steal their brother's whole shock than add to it a single sheaf!

BY GIVING IN THE MIDST OF OUR NEED,
WE OPEN OURSELVES TO TRUST IN
GOD'S PROVISION.

*J*OY OF *C*HRISTIANITY

*I*t does not make a man gloomy to become a child of God. See! There is a man going to execution. In a few moments he will be launched into eternity. But, flashing over the wires comes a message, a reprieve. I run in haste to the man. I shout, "Good news! Good news! You are not to die!" Does that make him gloomy? No! No! No! It is the want of Christ that makes men gloomy.

Take a man who is really thirsty, dying for want of water, and you go and give him water. Is that going to make him gloomy? That is what Christ is—water to the thirsty soul. If a man is dying for want of bread, and you give him bread, is that to make him gloomy? That is what Christ is to the soul—the bread of life. You will never have true pleasure or peace or joy or comfort until you have found Christ.

CHRIST IS INDEED LIFE;
REAL LIFE, FULL LIFE!

TURNING ON THE SEARCHLIGHT

When I was going through the land of Goshen in Egypt, a few years ago, as I came near the city of Alexandria, I saw the strangest sight I had ever seen. The heavens were lit up with a new kind of light, and there seemed to be flash after flash; I couldn't understand it. I had heard that the Khedive had died, and that a new Khedive was coming into power.

I found later that England had sent over some war vessels, and the moment that darkness came on they had turned their searchlights upon that city; it was almost as light as noonday.

Every street was lit up, and I do not suppose that ten men could have met in any part of Alexandria without being discovered by that searchlight.

May God turn His searchlight upon us, and see if there be any evil way in us!

•–•••–••–••–••–••–••–••–••–••–••–••–•••–•

GOD WILL TURN HIS SEARCHLIGHT ON US TO PURGE US OF EVIL.

THE ECHO

You may have heard of the boy whose home was in a wood. One day he thought he heard the voice of another boy not far off. He shouted, "Hallo, there!" and the voice shouted back, "Hallo, there!" He did not know that it was the echo of his own voice, and he shouted again: "You are a mean boy!" Again the cry came back, "You are a mean boy!"

After some more of the same kind of thing he went into the house and told his mother that there was a bad boy in the wood. His mother, who understood how it was, said to him:

"Oh, no! You speak kindly to him, and see if he does not speak kindly to you."

He went to the wood again and shouted, "Hallo, there!" "Hallo, there!" "You are a good boy." Of course the reply came, "You are a good boy." "I love you." "I love you," said the other voice.

This little story explains the secret of the whole thing. Some of you perhaps think you have bad and disagreeable neighbors; most likely the trouble is with yourself. If you love your neighbors they will love you. Love begets love.

GIVE LOVE AND YOU WILL
RECEIVE IT IN RETURN.

HARD TO BE COUNTERFEITED

A man can counterfeit love, he can counterfeit faith, he can counterfeit hope and all the other graces, but it is very difficult to counterfeit humility. You soon detect mock humility.

They have a saying in the East among the Arabs, that as the tares and the wheat grow they show which God has blessed. The ears that God has blessed bow their heads and acknowledge every grain, and the more fruitful they are the lower their heads are bowed. The tares which God has sent as a curse, lift up their heads erect, high above the wheat, but they are only fruitful of evil.

I have a pear tree on my farm which is very beautiful; it appears to be one of the most beautiful trees on my place. Every branch seems to be reaching up to the light and stands almost like a wax candle, but I never get any fruit from it. I have another tree, which was so full of fruit last year that the branches almost touched the ground.

If we only get down low enough, my friends, God will use every one of us to His glory.

AS WE BOW LOW BEFORE GOD HE WILL USE US FOR HIS GLORY.

THE HAUGHTY INFIDEL'S CHALLENGE

In the town of Hanover, Germany, I am told that there is buried a German countess who denied the existence of God and ridiculed the idea of the resurrection. To show her contempt for Christianity she ordered that on her death her grave should be built of solid masonry and covered by large stones bound together by iron clamps. On this tomb was engraved her defiant challenge that through eternity this tomb should never be disturbed.

One day a seed from some tree, either blown by the wind or carried by a bird, became lodged in a small crevice of the tomb, where soon it sprouted and began to grow. And then, as if Nature mocked the haughty infidel, she quietly extended the delicate roots of that seedling under the massive blocks of stone and slowly raised them from their place.

Although scarce four generations are passed since that tomb was sealed, that most insignificant seedling has accomplished what God Himself was challenged to accomplish.

●━━━━━━━━━━━━━━━●

GOD CAN USE THE SMALLEST OBJECT TO OVERCOME OUR LARGEST CHALLENGES.

HE HAD HIS EYES OPENED

The story is told of a boy whose parents took him to Florida to spend the winter. He returned to his city home, disgusted with the country he had been in. It was dull, stupid, and uninteresting, he said. During the next few months, however, he was in charge of a tutor who was an enthusiastic botanist, and he kindled the boy's interest in his favorite study. The boy learned about orchids, and their strange life. His tutor took him to a conservatory that he might see some of them growing.

"You should see them in Florida," the tutor said, "they are much better there; but these will give you an idea."

The boy looked at him in amazement.

"I have been in Florida," he said, "but I never noticed any of them.

"Perhaps you did not look for them," the tutor answered. "But they will not escape you the next time."

That is often the way with the Bible. A person sees no beauty in it, but the Holy Spirit is ready to open the eyes of our understanding and teach us. It may be by some sermon or book which will lift a truth out of its hiding place, and give it an application to our life it never had before.

THE HOLY SPIRIT IS READY TO OPEN OUR EYES TO THE TRUTH OF HIS WORD.

THE ILLUMINATION OF THE HOLY SPIRIT

I happened to be in Palestine some years ago. In the south part of the land, we had to go through some dry spots—fields quite dry—but we were told that if you were only to flood that ground with water, it would spring into verdure. There are plenty of seeds lying in the ground, dropped at various times—some of them dropped by the birds of the air—so that you have only to let a flood of water upon the field, and in a short time you will have a rush of life.

Now, it may be just like that in the case of some people. You have been taught the Word of God; you know the doctrines of the Word; you know them in your head, and, perhaps, approve of them, too; but they have no power over you, and you have no feeling. When, however, the Spirit comes, floods are poured over the dry field. What you knew before blossoms in new meaning. You wonder, "How did I not feel that before?" Or, you say, "I knew that, but I never saw the application of it before." It is because the Spirit has come.

WE SHOULD DAILY ASK THE LORD
TO FILL US ANEW WITH THE HOLY SPIRIT.

WANTED—A NEW SONG!

There was a Wesleyan preacher in England, Peter Mackenzie, full of native humor, a most godly man. He was once preaching from the text, "And They Sang a New Song," and he said:

"Yes, there will be singing in heaven, and when I get there I will want to have David with his harp, and Paul, and Peter and other saints gather around for a sing. And I will announce a hymn from the Wesleyan Hymnal. 'Let us sing hymn No. 749 —'

My God, my Father, while I stray—

"But someone will say, 'That won't do. You are in heaven, Peter; there's no straying here.' And I will say, 'Yes, that's so. Let us sing No. 651 —'

Though waves and storms go o'er my head,

Though friends be gone and hopes be dead—

"But another saint will interrupt, 'Peter, you forget you are in heaven now; there are no storms here.' 'Well, I will try again, No. 536 —'

Into a world of ruffians sent—

"'Peter! Peter!' someone will say, 'we will put you out unless you stop giving out inappropriate hymns.' I will ask— what can we sing? And they will all say:

"'Sing the new song, the song of Moses and the Lamb.'"

•—•—••—•—••—•—••—•—••—•—••—•—••—•—•

IN HEAVEN THE OLD HYMNS WILL BE INSUFFICIENT.

A Penalty Necessary

A person once said to me, "I hate your God; your God demands blood. I don't believe in such a God. My God is merciful to all. I do not know your God."

If you will turn to Leviticus 17:11, you will find why God demands blood: "For the life of the flesh is in the blood: and I have given it to you upon the altar to make an atonement for your souls; for it is the blood that maketh an atonement for the soul."

Suppose there was a law that man should not steal, but no penalty was attached to stealing; some man would have my pocketbook before dinner. If I threatened to have him arrested, he would snap his fingers in my face. He would not fear the law, if there was no penalty. It is not the law that people are afraid of; it is the penalty attached.

Do you suppose God has made a law without a penalty? What an absurd thing it would be! Now, the penalty for sin is death: "The soul that sinneth, it shall die." I must die, or get somebody to die for me. If the Bible doesn't teach that, it doesn't teach anything. And that is where the atonement of Jesus Christ comes in.

◆•••◆••◆••◆••◆••◆••◆••◆••◆••◆••◆••◆••◆••◆

LAWS THAT ARE DISOBEYED
ALWAYS HAVE CONSEQUENCES.

GIVE UP NOW!

Dr. Andrew Bonar told me how, in the Highlands of Scotland, a sheep would often wander off into the rocks and get into places that they couldn't get out of. The grass on these mountains is very sweet and the sheep like it, and they will jump down ten or twelve feet, and then they can't jump back again, and the shepherd hears them bleating in distress. They may be there for days, until they have eaten all the grass. The shepherd will wait until they are so faint they cannot stand, and then they will put a rope around him, and he will go over and pull that sheep out of the jaws of death.

"Why don't they go down there when the sheep first gets there?" I asked.

"Ah!" he said, "they are so very foolish they would dash right over the precipice and be killed if they did!"

And that is the way with men; they won't go back to God till they have no friends and have lost everything. If you are a wanderer I tell you that the Good Shepherd will bring you back the moment you have given up trying to save yourself and are willing to let Him save you His own way.

IF GOD DID NOT PULL US BACK WE WOULD FALL INTO OUR OWN DESTRUCTION.

*L*OOKING *D*OWNWARD

I heard once of a man who dreamed that he was swept into heaven, and oh, he was so delighted to think that he had at last got there. All at once one came and said:

"Come, I want to show you something."

He took him to the battlements, and he said, "Look down yonder; what do you see?"

"I see a very dark world."

"Look and see if you know it."

"Why, yes," he said, "that is the world I have come from."

"What do you see?"

"Men are blindfolded there; many of them are going over a precipice."

"Well, will you stay here and enjoy heaven, or will you go back to earth and spend a little longer time, and tell those men about this world?"

He was a Christian worker who had been discouraged. He awoke from his sleep and later he said:

"I have never wished myself dead since."

SEEING CLEARLY A NEEDY WORLD
MOTIVATES US TO SERVICE.

SCISSORS OR ORANGES?

My wife told me one day that she had just come from a friend's house where one of the children, a little boy, had been cutting something with a knife, and it had slipped upward and put out his eye, and his mother was afraid of his losing the other. Of course, after that my wife was careful that our little boy, two years old, shouldn't get the scissors, or anything by which he could harm himself. But prohibit a child from having any particular thing, and he's sure to have it. So one day our little fellow got hold of the scissors. His sister seeing what he had, and knowing the law, tried to take the scissors from him, but the more she tried the more he clung to them. All at once she remembered that he liked oranges, and that there was one in the next room. Away she went and back she came:

"Willie, would you like an orange?"

The scissors were dropped, and he clutched the orange.

God sometimes takes away the scissors, but He gives us an orange. Get both your feet into the narrow way; it leads to life and joy; its ways are the ways of pleasantness, and all its paths are peace. It is the way of victory, of peace; no gloom there; all light.

* * *

PUT YOURSELF ON THE NARROW PATH AND AVOID THOSE ATTRACTIVE THINGS THAT ARE HARMFUL.

It Seemed a Small Thing

I remember hearing of a man at sea who was very seasick. If there is a time when a man feels that he cannot do any work for the Lord it is then—in my opinion. While this man was sick he heard that a man had fallen overboard. He was wondering if he could do anything to help save him. He laid hold of a light and held it up to the porthole.

The drowning man was saved. When this man got over his attack of sickness he was up on deck one day, and was talking to the man who was rescued. The saved man gave this testimony. He said he had gone down the second time, and was just going down again for the last time, when he put out his hand. Just then, he said, someone held a light at the porthole, and the light fell on his hand. A man caught him by the hand and pulled him into the lifeboat.

It seemed a small thing to do to hold up the light, yet it saved the man's life. If you cannot do some great thing you can hold the light for some poor, perishing drunkard, who may be won to Christ and delivered from destruction. Let us take the torch of salvation and go into these dark homes, and hold up Christ to the people as the Savior of the world.

LET US LIFT UP HIGH THE LIGHT OF CHRIST
SO THE LOST CAN FIND THEIR WAY HOME.

THE UNERRING GUIDE

I am told by people who have been over the Alps, that the guide fastens them, if they are going in a dangerous place, right to himself, and he goes on before. And so should the Christian be linked to his unerring Guide, and be safely upheld.

If a man was going through the Mammoth Cave, it would be almost death to him if he strayed away from his guide. If separated from him, he would almost certainly perish. There are pitfalls in that cave, and a bottomless river, and there would be no chance for a man to find his way out of that cave without a guide or a light. So there is no chance for us to get through the dark wilderness of this world alone. It is folly for men and women to think that they can get through this evil world without the light of God's Word and the guidance of the divine Spirit. God sent Him to guide us through this great journey, and if we seek to work independent of Him, we shall stumble into the deep darkness of eternity's night.

•••••••••••••••••••••••••••••••

WE SHOULD FASTEN OURSELVES
TO CHRIST TO GET THROUGH
THE MOST DANGEROUS JOURNEY.

Lies Never Called Back

*T*he most dangerous thing about a lie is that a word once uttered can never be obliterated. Someone has said that lying is a worse crime than counterfeiting. There is some hope of following up bad coins until they are all recovered, but an evil word can never be overtaken. The mind of the hearer or reader has been poisoned, and human devices cannot reach in and cleanse it. Lies can never be called back.

A woman who was well-known as a scandalmonger, went and confessed to the priest. He gave her a ripe thistletop and told her to go out and scatter the seeds one by one. She wondered at the penance but obeyed, then she came and told the priest. He next told her to go and gather again the scattered seeds. Of course she saw that it was impossible. The priest used it as an object lesson to cure her of the sin of scandalous talk.

❖●═●═●═●═●═●═●═●═●═●═●═●═●❖

IT IS IMPOSSIBLE TO TAKE BACK
AND MAKE RIGHT THE EFFECTS OF
FALSEHOODS, GOSSIP, AND THE LIKE.

CLOGGED BY SAND

A number of years ago the mouth of the Mississippi River became so clogged that no vessels could pass through the channel. Much anxiety was felt, for the farmers along its banks depended upon the river for the transportation of their products.

There were no great, overhanging rocks to fall into the stream and block the way of the vessels. No volcanic upheaval had changed its bed. The trouble was simply the deposit of sediment—washings from the muddy banks and bottom of the river, so fine that a filter would hardly free the water from its impurity. And yet these tiny specks, massed together, hindered the great river's flow to the ocean, and for a time threatened the industries of the Southwestern states.

It does not take some great sin to block the channel of blessing. Small sins will block the stream.

Human ingenuity at last found a way to keep the Mississippi channel open, but only divine power can free our hearts from sin.

THE SMALL SINS OF OUR LIVES CAN GREATLY INHIBIT GOD'S PLAN IF THEY ARE NOT REPENTED OF AND DEALT WITH.

BOTH AFRAID

I remember a man in New York who used to come and pray with me. He had his cross. He was afraid to confess Christ. It seemed that down at the bottom of his trunk he had a Bible. He wanted to get it out and read it to a companion with whom he lived, but he was ashamed to do it. For a whole week that was his cross; and after he had carried the burden that long, and after a terrible struggle, he made up his mind, "I will take my Bible out tonight and read it." He took it out, and soon he heard the footsteps of his mate coming upstairs.

His first impulse was to put it away again, but then he thought he would not—he would face his companion with it. His mate came in, and seeing him at his Bible, said:

"John, are you interested in these things?"

"Yes," he replied.

"How long has this been, then?" asked his companion.

"Exactly a week," he answered. "For a whole week I have tried to get out my Bible to read to you, but I have never done so till now."

"Well," said his friend, "it is a strange thing. *I was converted on the same night,* and I, too, was ashamed to take my Bible out."

WE NEED TO ENCOURAGE EACH OTHER WHEN WE ARE HESITANT TO SHARE CHRIST WITH OTHERS.

THE OTHERS WERE SORRY

A Sunday school teacher wished to show his class how free the gift of God is. He took a silver watch from his pocket and offered it to the eldest boy in the class.

"It's yours, if you will take it."

The little fellow sat and grinned at the teacher. He thought he was joking. The teacher offered it to the next boy, and said:

"Take that watch, it is yours."

The little fellow thought he would be laughed at if he held out his hand, and therefore he sat still. In the same way the teacher went nearly around the class, but not one of them would accept the proffered gift. At length he came to the smallest boy. When the watch was offered to the little fellow, he took it and put it into his pocket. All the class laughed at him.

"I am thankful, my boy," said the teacher, "that you believe my word. The watch is yours. Take good care of it. Wind it up every night."

The rest of the class looked on in amazement, and one of them said, "Teacher, you don't mean that the watch is his? You don't mean that he hasn't to give it back to you?"

"No," said the teacher, "he hasn't to give it back to me. It is his own now."

"Oh — h — h! If I had only known that, wouldn't I have taken it!"

◆━◆━◆━◆━◆━◆━◆━◆━◆━◆━◆━◆━◆━◆━◆━◆━◆

SOME OFFERS SEEM TOO GOOD TO BE TRUE,
AND YET THE BEST ONES ARE TRUE.

THIS IS OUR HOPE

A bright young girl of fifteen was suddenly cast upon a bed of suffering, completely paralyzed on one side and nearly blind. She heard the family doctor say to her parents as they stood by the bedside—

"She has seen her best days, poor child!"

"No, doctor," she exclaimed, "my best days are yet to come, when I shall see the King in His beauty."

That is our hope. We shall not sink into annihilation. Christ rose from the dead to give us a pledge of our own rising. The resurrection is the great antidote for fear of death. Nothing else can take its place. Riches, genius, worldly pleasures or pursuits—none can bring us consolation in the dying hour. "All my possessions for a moment of time," cried Queen Elizabeth, when dying. "I have provided in the course of my life for everything except death, and now, alas! I am to die unprepared," were the last words of Cardinal Borgia. Compare with these last words of one of the early disciples, "I am weary. I will now go to sleep. Good night!" He had the sure hope of awaking in a brighter land.

THE LAST WORDS OF A PERSON OFTEN REFLECT THEIR PREPARATION FOR ETERNITY.

"THE PRECIOUS BLOOD"

One night, after a man had taken his seat, I noticed that his eyes looked as if he had been weeping. I gave out one hymn after another, all bearing on the Atonement, as that was the subject for the sermon. When I gave out the text, "The precious blood," I saw him cover his face and bow his head, and he wept aloud. He followed me into the inquiry room after the meeting was over, and said to me:

"Mr. Moody, this has been the most extraordinary day in my life. When I got up this morning the words 'Precious blood' came into my mind. When I went downtown to my place of business the words 'Precious blood' were ringing in my mind, and all during the day it was 'Precious blood, precious blood.' They followed me here tonight, and when you gave out your text, 'The precious blood,' I could hardly stay in my seat. I can't understand it."

"Well," I said, "I can." And after talking with him for a while he accepted Christ then and there. He is now dead, but when I was passing through that city years after I asked about him, they told me in all the years he had lived he had never lost his hold on Christ.

THE PRECIOUS BLOOD OF JESUS
PROVIDES THE MOST COMFORTING
ASSURANCE WE CAN KNOW.

Sincerity v. Truth

Some people tell you it makes no difference what you believe, if you are only sincere. I have heard lots of people say, "You do not think it makes any difference what a man's creed is, do you, if he is only sincere? The disciples of Mahomet and Confucius are all right if they are only sincere."

That is the biggest lie that ever came out of hell. A lie never lifted anyone yet. It is the truth that makes us free, and it is *that* which we want to believe. A lie does a man no good simply because he is sincere.

Suppose that I present a check for $10,000 at some bank, and the cashier says:

"Have you any money in this bank?"

I say, "No."

"Well," he says, "why are you trying to draw this money?"

I answer, "Well, I am very *sincere* about it, and I want $10,000 very much; I don't think any man wants it more than I do."

My earnestness will not get me that money. Some people get hold of a lie, and hold on to it. If you are wise, my friend, you will look and see if you believe the truth or not.

◆━◆━◆━◆━◆━◆━◆━◆━◆━◆━◆━◆━◆━◆━◆━◆

BEING EARNEST AND SINCERE WILL NEVER
SUBSTITUTE FOR THE WAY THINGS ARE,
RATHER THAN WHAT WE WANT THEM TO BE.

A Perfect Farce!

Here comes a man, and he admits that he gets drunk every week. That man comes to a meeting and wants to be converted. Shall I say, "Don't you be in a hurry. I believe in doing the work gradually. Don't you get drunk and knock your wife down more than once a month." Wouldn't it be refreshing to his wife to go a whole month without being knocked down? Once a month, only twelve times in a year! Wouldn't she be glad to have him converted in this new way! Only get drunk after a few years on the anniversary of your wedding, and at Christmas, and then it will be effective because it is gradual!

Oh! I detest all that kind of teaching. Let us go to the Bible and see what that old Book teaches. Let us believe it, and go and act as if we believed it, too. Salvation is instantaneous. I admit that a man may be converted so that he cannot tell when he crossed the line between death and life, but I also believe a man may be a thief one moment and a saint the next. I believe a man may be as vile as hell itself one moment and be saved the next.

SIN MUST CEASE IMMEDIATELY
RATHER THAN GRADUALLY, OR
IT WILL KEEP ITS HOLD ON YOU.

"GIVE HIM A CHEER!"

You have heard the story of the child who was rescued from the fire that was raging in a house way up in the fourth story. The child came to the window, and as the flames were shooting up higher and higher he cried out for help. A fireman started up the ladder of the fire escape to rescue the child from his dangerous position. The wind swept the flames near him, and it was getting so hot that he wavered, and it looked as if he would have to return without the child. Thousands looked on, and their hearts quaked at the thought of the child having to perish in the fire, as he must do if the fireman did not reach him. Someone in the crowd cried:

"Give him a cheer!"

Cheer after cheer went up, and as the man heard them he gathered fresh courage. Up he went into the midst of the smoke and the fire, and brought down the child in safety.

If you cannot go and rescue the perishing yourself, you can at least pray for those who do, and cheer them on. If you do, the Lord will bless the effort. Do not grumble and criticize; it takes neither heart nor brains to do that.

LET US PRAY FOR THOSE IN NEED OF SALVATION, WHETHER OR NOT WE ARE ABLE TO REACH THEM PERSONALLY.

Are You Sure?

After John Wesley had been preaching for some time, someone said to him, "Are you sure, Mr. Wesley, of your salvation?"

"Well," he answered, "Jesus Christ died for the whole world."

"Yes, we all believe that; but are you sure that *you* are saved?"

Wesley replied that he was sure that provision had been made for his salvation.

"But are you sure, Wesley, that *you* are saved?"

It went like an arrow to his heart, and he had no rest or power until that question was settled.

Many men and many women go on month after month, and year after year, without power, because they do not know their standing in Christ; they are not sure of their own footing for eternity. Latimer wrote Ridley once that when he was settled and steadfast about his own salvation he was as bold as a lion, but if that hope became eclipsed he was fearful and afraid and was disqualified for service. Many are disqualified for service because they are continually doubting their own salvation.

--◆--◆--◆--◆--◆--◆--◆--◆--◆--◆--◆--◆--◆--

MAKE SURE YOU KNOW YOU
ARE SAVED BEFORE SERVICE—
GOD WILL PROVIDE CERTAINTY.

IN HIS DRAWING ROOM

There was a young man in the middle west who had been more or less interested about his soul's salvation. One afternoon, in his office, he said:

"I will accept Jesus Christ as my Lord and Savior."

He went home and told his wife, who was a nominal professor of religion, that he had made up his mind to serve Christ, and he added:

"After supper tonight I am going to take the company into the drawing room and erect the family altar."

"Well," said his wife, "you know some of the gentlemen who are coming to tea are skeptics, and they are older than you are. Don't you think you had better wait until after they have gone, or else go out in the kitchen and have your first prayer with the servants?"

The young man thought for a few moments, and then he said:

"I have asked Jesus Christ into my house for the first time, and I shall take Him into the best room, not into the kitchen."

So he called his friends into the drawing room. There was a little sneering, but he read and prayed. That man afterward became Chief Justice of the United States Court.

Never be ashamed of the gospel of Christ; it is the power of God unto salvation.

<hr />

GOD WILL GRANT SUCCESS TO THOSE WHO PUT HIM FIRST IN THEIR FAMILY.

MAN'S IDEA OF GRACE

Men talk about grace, but, as a rule, they know very little about it. Let a businessman go to one of your bankers to borrow a few hundred dollars for sixty or ninety days. If he is well able to pay, the banker will perhaps lend him the money if he can get another responsible man to sign the note with him. They give what they call "three days' grace" after the sixty or ninety days have expired; but they will make the borrower pay interest on the money during these three days, and if he does not return principal and interest at the appointed time, they will sell his goods. They will perhaps turn him out of his house, and take the last piece of furniture in his possession.

That is not grace at all, but that fairly illustrates man's idea of it. Grace not only frees you from payment of the interest, but of the principal also. The grace of God frees us from the penalty of our sin without any payment on our part. Christ has paid the debt, and all we have to do is to believe on Him for our salvation.

GOD PAYS OUR DEBTS—
BOTH PRINCIPAL AND INTEREST.

THEY ALL BLACKBALLED HIM

There was a sailor whose mother had long been praying for him. One night the memory of his mother came home to this man. He thought of the days of his childhood, and made up his mind he would try and lead a different life. When he got to New York he thought he would join the Odd Fellows; he imagined that would be a good way to begin. What miserable mistakes men make when they get trying to save themselves! This man applied to a lodge of Odd Fellows for admission; but the committee found that he was a drinking man, and so they blackballed him. Then he thought he would try the Freemasons; they discovered what sort of a man he was, and they blackballed him, too.

One day he was walking along Fulton Street, when he received an invitation to come to the daily prayer meeting held there. He went in, and heard about the Savior. He received Christ into his heart, and found the peace and power he wanted. Some days after he stood up in the meeting and told his story—how the Odd Fellows had blackballed him; how the Freemasons had blackballed him; and how he came to the Lord Jesus Christ, Who had not blackballed him, but took him right in.

THOUGH HUMAN ORGANIZATIONS MAY FIND FAULT WITH US, GOD ACCEPTS US AS SINNERS, BECAUSE HE TOOK OUR SIN AWAY.

*S*HE MADE A *M*ISTAKE

*D*octor Arnot was accustomed to tell a story of a poor woman who was in great distress because she could not pay her landlord his rent. The doctor put some money in his pocket, and went round to her house, intending to help her. When he got there he knocked at the door. He thought he heard some movement inside, but no one came to open the door. He knocked louder and louder still, but yet no one came. Finally he kicked at the door, causing some of the neighbors to look out and see what was going on, but he could get no entrance. At last he went away, thinking his ears must have deceived him, and that there was really no one there.

A day or two afterward he met the woman in the street, and told her what had happened. She held up her hands and exclaimed:

"Was that you? I was in the house all the while, but I thought it was the landlord, and I had the door locked!"

Many people think the grace of God is coming to smite them. My dear friends, it is coming to pay all your debts!

SOME OF US CANNOT ACCEPT THE IDEA OF
THE FREE GRACE OF GOD BECAUSE IT
SEEMS TOO GOOD TO BE TRUE.

*G*OD IS NOT *D*EAD

*T*he story is told that Frederick Douglass, the great slave orator, once said in a mournful speech when things looked dark for his race:

"The white man is against us, governments are against us, the spirit of the times is against us. I see no hope for the colored race. I am full of sadness."

Just then a poor old colored woman rose in the audience, and said:

"Frederick, is God dead?"

Now, many a young believer is discouraged and disheartened when he realizes this warfare. He begins to think that God has forsaken him, that Christianity is not all that it professes to be. But he should rather regard it as an encouraging sign. No sooner has a soul escaped from his snare than the great adversary takes steps to ensnare it again. He puts forth all his powers to recapture his lost prey. The fiercest attacks are made on the strongest forts, and the fiercer the battle the young believer is called on to wage, the surer evidence it is of the work of the Holy Spirit in his heart. God will not desert him in his time of need.

THE ADVERSARY WILL TRY TO RECLAIM US,
BUT GOD WILL NOT DESERT US.

A TRAGIC ENDING

At one place where I went to hold meetings it was advertised in the papers that I was going to stay thirty days. Now, there was a lady who was a member of one of the churches, and she said:

"I don't want to have my boy brought under the influence of those meetings. I'm afraid he'll be brought into the Young Men's Christian Association, and they'll have him out on the streets with tracts, and it would be very mortifying to me to have my son doing such a thing as that."

She was ambitious for her boy, and wanted to get him into the bon-ton society, as they call it. So she planned to take her son out of the city, and to be gone for those thirty days. She told her pastor why she had taken him, but I knew nothing about it.

The meetings went on, and just at my right hand sat that minister, from the beginning till the end, until the last meeting, when he was absent. Just as the benediction was pronounced, and the people were about to leave, he came rushing in and said he was so sorry he had not been there.

"I have just been called on one of the saddest errands of my life," he said, and went on to tell me that that mother who had taken her son away from the influence of those meetings had brought him back that day in his coffin, and he had just come from the funeral.

WE HAVE A LIMITED AMOUNT OF TIME
TO GIVE OURSELVES WHOLLY TO GOD—
HALFWAY WILL NOT DO.

ALL PEOPLE ARE GUILTY

*I*n Chicago, when our City Constitution was new, a bill was passed that no man should be a policeman who was not a certain height—five feet six. The commissioners advertised for men to come round and be examined, and they must bring good letters of recommendation with them. Now as they are passing from one man to another, examining their letters, and trying their height, suppose there are two of us who want to get in, and I say to my friend, "There is no man has a better chance than I have; I have got letters from the supreme judge, from the mayor and leading citizens of Chicago; no man can have better letters." He says, "Ah, my friend, my letters are as good as yours."

Well, the chief commissioner says, "Look here, Moody, these letters are all right, but you must be up to the standard." And so he measures me, and I am only five feet, and he says, "You are half a foot too short." My friend looks down on me and says, "I have got a better chance than you." Well, he stands up and is measured, and is only one-tenth of an inch short, but he goes with me. He has come short. I admit some men have come shorter than others, but that is the verdict God has brought in—all are guilty.

ALL OF US FALL SHORT OF GOD'S STANDARDS. YES, WE ARE GUILTY.

THIS YOUNG MAN MADE A MISTAKE

In 1872, when I was coming back from Europe, there were a number of ministers on board. A young man who had evidently crossed several times before and knew the captain, stepped up to him and in a loud tone of voice, intending doubtless to insult some of the ministers, said he was sorry he had taken passage on the boat, as it would be unlucky to travel with so many parsons. The captain was himself a pretty rough fellow, and turning to him he said:

"If you'll show me a town in England where there are five thousand people and not one parson, I'll show you a place a mile nearer hell than ever you've been."

The young man walked away. I'd like to take all these people who do not believe in these things and put them on an island by themselves. Why, they'd sink the first boat that touched there in their efforts to get on board and get away!

THE WORLD WITHOUT THE INFLUENCE OF THE CHURCH IS THE NEAREST THING TO HELL.

THE SWAN AND THE CRANE

"Where do you come from?"

"I come from heaven!" replied the swan.

"And where is heaven?" asked the crane.

"Heaven!" said the swan, "heaven! Have you never heard of heaven?" And the beautiful bird went on to describe the grandeur of the Eternal City. She told of streets of gold, and the gates and walls made of precious stones; of the river of life, pure as crystal, upon whose banks is the tree whose leaves shall be for the healing of the nations. In eloquent terms the swan sought to describe the hosts who live in the other world, but without arousing the slightest interest on the part of the crane.

Finally the crane asked: "Are there any snails there?"

"Snails!" repeated the swan, "No! Of course there are not."

"Then," said the crane, as it continued its search along the slimy banks of the pool, "you can have your heaven. I want snails!"

This fable has a deep truth underlying it. How many a young person to whom God has granted the advantages of a Christian home, has turned his back upon it and searched for snails!

◆━•◆•━•◆•━•◆•━•◆•━•◆•━•◆•━•◆•━•◆•━•◆•━•◆

WE OFTEN SETTLE FOR FAR LESS THAN GOD INTENDS FOR US.

DON'T CALL ME A BEGGAR

Mr. Morehouse once used an illustration which fastened itself on my mind. He said:

Suppose you go up the street and meet a man whom you have known for the last ten years to be a beggar, and you notice a change in his appearance, and you say:

"Hello, beggar, what's come over you?"

"I ain't no beggar. Don't call me a beggar."

"Why," you say, "I saw you the other day begging in the street."

"Ah, but a change has taken place," he replies.

"Is that so? How did it come about?"

"Well," he says, "I came out this morning, and got down here intending to catch the businessmen and get money out of them, when one of them came up to me and said there was $10,000 deposited for me in the bank."

"How do you know this is true?" you say.

"I went to the bank and they put the money in my hand."

"Are you sure of that?" you ask. "How do you know it was the right kind of a hand?"

But he says, "I don't care whether it was the right kind of a hand or not; I got the money, and that's all I wanted."

Faith is the hand that reaches out and takes the blessing. Any faith that brings you to Christ is the right kind of faith, and instead of looking at your faith look to Christ.

WITH CHRIST WE ARE RICH, SO LET US
PUT OUR FAITH IN HIM BECAUSE
HE SUPPLIES ALL OUR NEEDS.

About Forgiveness

*S*uppose that I have a little boy, and when I go home he comes to me and says, "Papa, I did that naughty thing you told me not to do."

I see there are signs of contrition, and say, "I am sorry you did it, but I am thankful you confessed it. I forgive you."

He goes off lightly. He has been forgiven. But the next day he comes and says:

"Papa, do you know that yesterday while you were away I did that naughty thing that you told me not to do. I am very sorry. Won't you forgive me?"

I say, "My son, was not that forgiven yesterday?"

"Well," he says, "I wish you would forgive me again."

Don't you see how dishonoring it is? It is very disheartening to a father to have a child act in that way. And it is distrusting God, and dishonoring Him for us to be constantly lugging up the past. If God has forgiven us, that is the end of it.

JUST AS WE FORGIVE OUR CHILDREN
ONCE AND FOR ALL, SO GOD FORGIVES US.

"THEY LOVE A FELLOW OVER THERE!"

Show me a church where there is love, and I will show you a church that is a power in the community. In Chicago a few years ago a little boy attended a Sunday school I know of. When his parents moved to another part of the city the little fellow still attended the same Sunday school, although it meant a long, tiresome walk each way. A friend asked him why he went so far, and told him that there were plenty of other churches just as good nearer his home.

"They may be as good for others, but not for me," was his reply.

"Why not?" she asked.

"Because they love a fellow over there," he replied.

If only we could make the world believe that we loved them there would be fewer empty churches, and a smaller proportion of our population who never darken a church door. Let love replace duty in our church relations, and the world will soon be evangelized.

⟡•⟡•⟡•⟡•⟡•⟡•⟡•⟡•⟡•⟡•⟡•⟡•⟡•⟡•⟡

THE COMMAND TO LOVE ONE ANOTHER WAS MEANT TO REACH OUTSIDE THE CHURCH.

GOD HAD MOVED HIM

There was an ex-judge in Chicago who thought that requests for prayer were too sacred to be made public, and he disliked my way of asking God's aid for those in need.

He had a son who was with Grant at the siege of Richmond.

One morning he became particularly depressed in spirit as his thoughts went out to the boy. He could not shake off the feeling that something was going to happen to his son, and he went to the meeting, and after much hesitation, asked me to pray for him.

As he left the hall a telegram was handed to him. His son had been mortally wounded in battle that day. He said to me afterward that he firmly believed God put it into his head to come and ask for prayer.

LISTEN TO THE PROMPTINGS OF GOD,

FOR YOU MAY NOT HAVE THE SAME

OPPORTUNITY AGAIN.

EARNESTNESS IN PRAYER

"*T*eacher," said a bright, earnest-faced boy, "why is it that so many prayers are unanswered? I do not understand. The Bible says, 'Ask, and ye shall receive; seek, and ye shall find; knock, and it shall be opened unto you'; but it seems to me a great many knock and are not admitted." "Did you never sit by your fireplace," said the teacher, "on some dark evening and hear a loud knocking at the door? Going to answer the knock, have you not sometimes looked out into the darkness, seeing nothing, but hearing the pattering feet of some mischievous boy, who knocked but did not wish to enter, and therefore ran away? It is often so with us. We ask for blessings, but do not really expect them; we knock, but do not mean to enter; we fear that Jesus will not hear us, will not fulfill His promises, will not admit us; and so we go away."

"Ah, I see," said the earnest-faced boy, his eyes shining with the new light dawning in his soul. "Jesus can't be expected to answer runaway knocks. He has never promised it. I mean to keep knocking, knocking, until He can't help opening the door."

•◆•—•◆•—•◆•—•◆•—•◆•—•◆•—•◆•—•◆•—•◆•—•◆•

LET US PERSEVERE IN EARNEST PRAYER.

"YE ARE MY WITNESSES"

A friend of mine in Philadelphia was going by a drinking saloon one night, and he saw in that saloon a professed Christian playing cards. He took a pencil, wrote on a card, and saw a little boy and said:

"My boy, here is some money. I want you to do an errand for me. You see that man on the side of the table where those three are, playing cards with them?"

"Yes, I do."

"Well," said my friend, "take that card to him."

The boy went in, and my friend watched the man when this card was handed to him. What was written on the card was, "Ye are My witnesses." The man took the card, looked at it, sprang to his feet, and rushing out into the street asked the boy where the card came from. The boy said:

"A man over there gave it to me."

But the man had slipped away. "Ye are My witnesses." Wherever you find a professed Christian going in bad company, you may look for something worse.

———————————————

OUR BEHAVIOR WITNESSES TO THE QUALITY OF OUR CHRISTIAN LIFE.

THEY DID NOT HEED THE SIGNAL

I was in the north of England in 1881, when a fearful storm swept over that part of the country. A friend of mine, who was a minister at Eyemouth, had a great many of the fishermen of the place in his congregation. It had been very stormy weather, and the fishermen had been detained in the harbor for a week. One day, however, the sun shone out in a clear blue sky. It seemed as if the storm had passed away, and the boats started out for the fishing ground. Forty-one boats left the harbor that day. Before they started, the harbor master hoisted the storm signal, and warned them of the coming tempest. He begged of them not to go, but they disregarded his warning, and away they went. They saw no sign of the coming storm. In a few hours, however, it swept down on that coast, and very few of those fishermen returned. There were five or six men in each boat, and nearly all were lost in that dreadful gale.

Those men were ushered into eternity because they did not give heed to the warning. I lift up the storm signal now, and warn you to escape from the coming judgment!

◆••◆••◆••◆••◆••◆••◆••◆••◆••◆••◆••◆••◆••◆••◆

THERE ARE MANY SIGNS IN LIFE
SIGNIFYING ETERNAL DANGER. GOD
PROVIDES THEM SO WE MAY ESCAPE.

HE TRUSTED HIS FATHER

I was standing with a friend at his garden gate one evening when two little children came by. As they approached us he said to me:

"Watch the difference in these two boys."

Taking one of them in his arms he stood him on the gatepost, and stepping back a few feet he folded his arms and called to the little fellow to jump. In an instant the boy sprang toward him and was caught in his arms. Then turning to the second boy he tried the same experiment. But in the second case it was different. The child trembled and refused to move. My friend held out his arms and tried to induce the child to trust his strength, but nothing could move him. At last my friend had to lift him down from the post and let him go.

"What makes such a difference in the two?" I asked.

My friend smiled and said, "The first is my own boy and knows me, but the other is a stranger's child whom I have never seen before."

There was all the difference. My friend was equally able to prevent both from falling, but the difference was in the boys themselves. The first had assurance in his father's ability and acted upon it, while the second, although he might have believed in the ability to save him from harm, would not put his belief into action.

DO YOU HAVE THE ASSURANCE THAT YOUR FATHER WILL BE THERE TO KEEP YOU FROM HARM—TRUST HIM.

*L*OTS OF *P*EOPLE LIKE *H*IM

A friend of mine told me some years ago that his wife was very fond of painting, but that for a long time he never could see any beauty in her paintings; they all looked like a daub to him. One day his eyes troubled him, and he went to see an oculist. The man looked in amazement at him, and said:

"You have what we call a short eye and a long eye, and that makes everything a blur."

He gave him some glasses that just fit him, and then he could see clearly. Then he understood why it was that his wife was so carried away with art, and he went and built an art gallery, and filled it full of beautiful things, because everything looked so beautiful after he had had his eyes straightened out.

Now there are lots of people who have a long eye and a short eye, and they make miserable work of their Christian life. They keep one eye on the eternal city and the other eye on the well-watered plains of Sodom, and they have no happiness or enjoyment in either.

***

LET US KEEP OUR EYES SINGLY FOCUSED, THE LONG EYE LOOKING TOWARD HEAVEN.

*B*EST OF *A*LL

A Jewish rabbi once asked his scholars what was the best thing a man could have in order to keep him in the straight path. One said *a good disposition;* another, *a good companion;* another said *wisdom* was the best thing he could desire. At last a scholar replied that he thought *a good heart* was best of all.

"True," said the rabbi, "you have comprehended all that the others have said. For he that hath a good heart will be of a good disposition, and a good companion, and a wise man. Let everyone, therefore, cultivate a sincerity and uprightness of heart at all times, and it will save him an abundance of sorrow."

We need to make the prayer of David our prayer: "Create in me a clean heart, O God, and renew a right spirit within me!"

A GOOD AND PURE HEART IS
MORE IMPORTANT THAN ANY
OTHER VIRTUE OR TRAIT.

LIVING CHRIST

I said to a Scotchman one day as he stayed to the after meeting, "Would you speak to that young man there?"

He was a great manufacturer. He said, "Mr. Moody, I am very reticent; I don't know that I could do that."

I said, "Perhaps you can help him; I wish you would speak to him."

He sat down beside the young man and found him to be a workingman. He said that every Saturday noon when he was paid off and went home to get his dinner, a terrible thirst for strong drink came on him, and that by Monday all his wages were drunk up.

This gentleman asked, "What time do you get your dinner?"

He told him. The next Saturday afternoon that great manufacturer was there, and spent the whole afternoon with him. The next Saturday he came again, and he kept at it until he got that man away from the power of strong drink.

That is a good way to confess Christ. If you can't do it with your lips, you can do it in some way. Watch for opportunities to let the world know on whose side you stand.

THERE ARE MANY WAYS TO CONFESS CHRIST TO A LOST WORLD.

A Fragrant Act

One day a minister found a little boy, only six years old, who had been brought over from Fife. The little fellow was in great distress because the doctors were coming to take off his leg. Think how you would feel, if you had a little brother six years old and he was taken off to the hospital, and the doctor said that he was coming forty-eight hours afterward to take off his leg!

Well, that minister tried to comfort the boy, and said, "Your father will come to be with you."

"No," he said, "my father is dead. He cannot be here."

"Well, your mother will come."

"My mother is over in Fife. She is sick and cannot come."

The minister himself could not come, so he said, "Well, you know the matron here is a mother; she has got a great big heart."

The little chin began to quiver as the boy said, "Perhaps Jesus will be with me."

Do you have any doubt of it? Next Friday the man of God went to the hospital, but he found the cot was empty. The poor boy was gone. The Savior had come and taken him to His bosom.

One little act of kindness will often live a good deal longer than a most magnificent sermon.

SMALL ACTS OF KINDNESS MAKE A LARGE DIFFERENCE.

*P*RAYER FOR *C*HILDREN

I received a letter from Scotland. It was from a father. He asked us to look out for his boy, whose name was Willie. That name touched my heart, because it was the name of my own boy. I asked Mr. Sawyer to try and get on the track of that boy some weeks ago, but all his efforts were fruitless. But away off in Scotland that Christian father was holding his son up to God in prayer, and last Friday, in yonder room, among those asking for prayer was Willie. He told me a story that thrilled my heart, and testified how the prayers of that father and mother in a far-off land had been instrumental in affecting his salvation.

Don't you think the heart of that father and mother will rejoice? He said he was rushing madly to destruction, but there was a power in those prayers that saved that boy. Don't you think, my friends, that God hears and answers prayers, and shall we not lift up our voices to Him in prayer that He will bless the children He has given to us?

GOD HEARS AND ANSWERS ALL PRAYERS
OF HIS FAITHFUL FOLLOWERS.

THE IMPORTANCE OF CONTENTMENT

*I*ra Sankey, D. L. Moody's song leader, told of an incident that had occurred in his home in Brooklyn one Christmas, while he was in San Francisco. His little boy awoke about 4 o'clock in the morning, and got up to see what was in his stocking. He found a box of paints and a little book. He said, "Santa Claus knew just what I wanted," and went off contentedly to sleep.

When he arose at the usual time he was shown in a lower room a whole tree full of presents for him. He was satisfied with the trifles which he thought were all he was to get, and what was the joy of the mother to lead him into the place where greater things were prepared for him. When Christians are grateful for what they have already received, the Lord delights to give them far greater blessings.

BEING CONTENT AND GRATEFUL
WHERE THE LORD HAS PLACED US
IS OF GREAT HONOR TO GOD.

"It's Better Higher Up!"

She lived up in the garret, five stories up, and when they had got to the first story the lady drew up her dress, and said:

"How dark and filthy it is!"

"It's better higher up," said her friend.

They got to the next story, and it was no better; the lady complained again, but her friend replied:

"It's better higher up."

At the third floor it seemed still worse, and the lady kept complaining, but her friend kept saying:

"It's better higher up."

At last they got to the fifth story, and when they went into the sickroom, there was a nice carpet on the floor, flowering plants in the window, and little birds singing. And there they found this bedridden saint—one of those saints whom God is polishing for His own temple—just beaming with joy.

The lady said to her, "It must be very hard for you to lie here."

She smiled, and said, *"It's better higher up."*

Yes! And if things go against us, my friends, let us remember that "it's better higher up."

·—·—··—··—··—··—··—··—··—··—·—·

EVEN IN OUR TRIALS WE SHOULD KEEP OUR EYES UPWARD.

THEY DID NOT BELIEVE HIM

*A*bout ten o'clock a man was walking in front of the office. He looked this way and that to see if anybody was looking, and by and by, satisfied that there was no one looking, he slipped in, and said:

"I saw a notice about town that if anyone would call here at a certain hour you would pay their debts; is there any truth in it?"

"Yes," said the man; "it's quite true. Did you bring the necessary papers with you?"

"Yes."

After the man had paid the debt, he said, "Sit down, I want to talk with you," and he kept him there until twelve o'clock. Before twelve o'clock had passed two more came in and had their debts paid. At twelve o'clock he let them all out. Some other men were standing around the door.

"Well, did he pay your debts?"

"Yes," they said. "It was quite true, our debts were all paid."

"Oh! Then we'll go in and get ours paid."

They went, but it was too late. Twelve o'clock had passed. To every one of you who is a bankrupt sinner—and you never saw a sinner in the world who was not a bankrupt sinner—Christ comes and He says, "I will pay your debts."

WE ARE ALL BANKRUPT SINNERS BUT OUR DEBTS CAN ALL BE PAID.

THE INVITATION TO A SALOON OPENING

As a joke a saloon owner sent me an invitation to go to the opening. I took the invitation and went down and saw the two men who had the saloon, and I said:

"Is that a genuine invitation?"

They said it was.

"Thank you," I said, "I will be around, and if there is anything here I don't like, I may have something to say about it."

They said, "You are not going to *preach,* are you?"

"I may."

"We don't want you. We won't let you in."

"How are you going to keep me out?" I asked. "There is the invitation."

"We will put a policeman at the door."

"What is the policeman going to do with that invitation?"

"We won't let you in."

"Well," I said, "I will be there."

I gave them a good scare, and then I said, "I will compromise the matter; if you two men will get down here and let me pray with you, I will let you off."

I got those two rum sellers down on their knees, and I prayed God to save their souls and smite their business. After I had prayed, I said:

"How can you do this business? How can you throw this place open to ruin the young men of Chicago?"

Within three months the whole thing smashed up, and one of them was converted shortly after. I have never been invited to a saloon since.

◆◆◆◆◆◆◆◆◆◆◆◆◆◆◆◆◆◆

BRING YOUR PRAYERS AND CHRISTIAN WITNESS INTO THE PLACES OF THOSE WHO NEED IT MOST.

How One Man Treated Doubts

This man thought it was too simple and easy.

At last light seemed to break in upon him, and he seemed to find comfort from it. It was past midnight before he got down on his knees, but down he went and was converted. I said:

"Now, don't think you are going to get out of the devil's territory without trouble. The devil will come to you tomorrow morning and say it was all feeling, that you only imagine you were accepted by God. When he does, don't fight him with your own opinions, but fight him with John 6:37: 'Him that cometh to me I will in no wise cast out.' Let that be 'the sword of the Spirit.'"

I don't believe that any man ever starts to go to Christ but the devil strives somehow or other to meet him and trip him up. And even after he has come to Christ, the devil tries to assail him with doubts, and make him believe there is something wrong in it.

The struggle came sooner than I thought in this man's case. When he was on his way home the devil assailed him. He used this text, but the devil put this thought into his mind:

"How do you know Christ ever said that after all? Perhaps the translators made a mistake."

Into darkness he went again. He was in trouble till about two in the morning. At last he came to this conclusion. Said he:

"I will believe it anyway; and when I get to heaven, if it isn't true, I will just tell the Lord *I* didn't make the mistake—the translators made it."

TRUST GOD AT HIS WORD AND LET HIM SORT OUT THE DIFFICULTIES.

THE TREATMENT OF PARENTS

*T*ell me how you treat your parents, and I will tell you how your children will treat you. A man was making preparations to send his old father to the poorhouse, when his little child came up and said, "Papa, when you are old shall I have to take you to the poorhouse?"

Do you never write home to your parents? They clothed you and educated you, and now do you spend your nights in gambling? You say to your godless companions that your father crammed religion down your throat when you were a boy. I have a great contempt for a man who says that of his father or mother.

They may have made a mistake, but it was of the head, not of the heart. If a telegram was sent to them that you were down with smallpox, they would take the first train to come to you. They would willingly take the disease into their own bodies and die for you. If you scoff and sneer at your father and mother you will have a hard harvest; you will reap in agony. It is only a question of time. There is a saying—

> The mills of God grind slowly,
>
> But they grind exceeding small.
>
> With patience He stands waiting,
>
> With exactness grinds He all.

❖❖❖❖❖❖❖❖❖❖❖❖❖❖❖❖❖❖❖

HONOR YOUR PARENTS, FOR THEY WERE GIVEN TO YOU BY GOD.

THE LITTLE LONE ONE

I sometimes think if an angel were to wing its way to heaven, and tell them that there was one little child here on earth—it might be a shoeless, coatless street Arab—with no one to lead it to the cross of Christ, and if God were to call the angels round His throne and ask them to go and spend, aye, fifty years, in teaching that child, there would not be an angel in heaven but would respond gladly to the appeal. We should see even Gabriel saying, "Let me go and win that soul to Christ." We should see Paul buckling on his old armor again, and saying, "Let me go back again to earth, that I may have the joy of leading that little one to his Savior."

Ah! We need rousing; there is too much apathy amongst professing Christians. Let us pray God that He may send His Holy Spirit to inspire us with fresh energy and zeal to do His work.

THERE ARE SO MANY LITTLE LOST
SOULS TO CAPTURE FOR CHRIST—
LET US GET TO WORK!

THE RIGHT TIME FOR ACTION

A man was always telling his servant that he was going to do a great thing for him. "I am going to remember you in my will."

Sam got his expectations up very high. When the man came to die, it was found that all he had willed Sam was to be buried in the family plot. That was the big thing, you know. Sam said he wished he had given him ten dollars, and let the lot go.

If you want to show kindness to a person, show it to him while he is living. I heard a man say that he didn't want people to throw bouquets to him after he was dead, and say, "There, smell them."

Now, this is the time for action. I have got so tired and sick of this splitting hairs over theology. Man, let us go out and get the fallen up. Lift them up toward God and heaven. We want a practical kind of Christianity.

THEOLOGY IS IMPORTANT, BUT LET'S NOT NEGLECT THOSE WHO ARE PERISHING BECAUSE WE ARGUE ABOUT DOCTRINE.

THE TRUE SOURCE OF JOY

God doesn't ask us to rejoice over nothing; He gives us ground for our joy. What would you think of a man who seemed very happy today and full of joy, and couldn't tell you what made him so? Suppose I should meet a man on the street, and he was so full of joy that he should get hold of both my hands and say:

"Bless the Lord, I am so full of joy!"

"What makes you so full of joy?"

"Well, I don't know."

"You don't know!"

"No, I don't; but I am so joyful that I just want to get out of the flesh."

"What makes you feel so joyful?"

"Well, I don't know."

Would we not think such a person unreasonable? But there are a great many people who want to feel that they are Christians before they are Christians; they want to have the joy of the Lord before they receive Jesus Christ. But this is not the gospel order. He brings joy when He comes, and we cannot have joy apart from Him. He is the author of it, and we find our joy in Him.

JESUS CHRIST HIMSELF IS OUR JOY.
WE CANNOT FIND JOY EXCEPT IN HIM.

*U*NITY

*T*here is one thing I have noticed as I have traveled in different countries; I never yet have known the Spirit of God to work where the Lord's people were divided. Unity is one thing that we must have if we are to have the Holy Spirit of God to work in our midst.

If a church is divided, the members should immediately seek unity. Let the believers come together and get the difficulty out of the way. If the minister of a church cannot unite the people, if those who were dissatisfied will not fall in, it would be better for that minister to retire. I think there are a good many ministers in this country who are losing their time; they have lost, some of them, months and years; they have not seen any fruit, and they will not see any fruit, because they have a divided church. Such a church cannot grow in divine things. The Spirit of God doesn't work where there is division, and what we want today is the spirit of unity amongst God's children, so that the Lord may work.

THE SPIRIT OF GOD DOESN'T WORK WHERE THERE ARE DIVIDED HEARTS.

GETTING ON SPLENDIDLY

One man said to another, some time ago, "How are you getting on at your church?"

"Oh, splendid."

"Many conversions?"

"Well—well, on that side we are not getting on so well. But," he said, "we have rented all our pews and are able to pay all our running expenses. We are getting on splendidly."

That is what the godless call "getting on splendidly." They rent the pews, pay the minister, and meet all the running expenses.

A man was being shown through one of the cathedrals of Europe; he had come in from the country. One of the men belonging to the cathedral was showing him around, when he inquired:

"Do you have many conversions here?"

"Many what?"

"Many conversions here?"

"Ah, man, this is not a Wesleyan chapel."

The idea of there being conversions there! And you can go into a good many churches in this country and ask if they have many conversions there, and they would not know what it meant. They are so far away from the Lord, they are not looking for conversions, and don't expect them.

◆━■━◆━■━◆━■━◆━■━◆━■━◆━■━◆━■━◆

THE WORST BOOK TO NEGLECT IS THE BIBLE.

*P*RAISE FOR *H*EALTH

There was a poor, afflicted man living in Chicago, and I never came out of his house without praising God. He was deaf, dumb, blind, and had lockjaw. He had a hole between his teeth, and all the food he took was put through that hole. My friend, do you ever thank God for your senses? Do you ever thank God for your eyes, by which you can read the Bible? Think of the millions of people in this world who haven't any sight at all. Hundreds of thousands of them never saw the mother who gave them birth; never saw their own offspring; never saw nature in all its glory; never saw the beautiful sun and the stars. Do you ever praise God for the ears by which you can hear the voice of man, by which you hear the gospel preached, by which you hear the songs of God's praise? Do you ever praise God for your own reasons?

•••••••••••••••••••••••••••••••

FORGIVE US FOR NOT THANKING YOU,
LORD GOD, FOR ALL YOUR BLESSINGS.

THE PROMISE FOR ALL

Every one of God's proclamations is connected with that word "whosoever"—"whosoever believeth," "whosoever will." I think it was Richard Baxter who said he thanked God for that "whosoever."

I heard of a woman once who thought there was no promise in the Bible for her; she thought the promises were for someone else, not for her. There are a good many of these people in the world. They think it is too good to be true that they can be saved for nothing. This woman one day got a letter, and when she opened it she found it was not for her at all; it was meant for another woman who had the same name. She had her eyes opened to the fact that if she should find some promise in the Bible directed to her name, she would not know whether it meant her or someone else that bore her name. But you know the word "whosoever" includes everyone in the wide world.

◆•❖•❖•❖•❖•❖•❖•❖•❖•❖•❖•❖•❖•❖•◆•

"WHOSOEVER" MEANS NOT JUST ANYONE,
BUT YOU, IF YOU WILL COME TO CHRIST.

THE EXAMPLE OF FAMILY ALTAR

A businessman in Edinburgh, Scotland, came to our meeting. He had made up his mind that he ought to live right as a Christian and he ought to have a family altar. And as he hurried his wife and children up the next morning, his wife said, "George, what's your hurry?"

He replied, "I have a confession to make this morning, and I want all of you to forgive me. You have never heard me say any words in prayer. I am going to start this morning. I want you and the children to help me." And he got down on his knees and confessed his soul as well as he could.

I do not know of a man who was ever more blessed of God than that man. God responded to the urgent desire of his heart. Do you need to make a similar decision of commitment to God for yourself and your family? God will meet you and bless you.

GOD BLESS OUR HOMES WITH
YOUR PRESENCE AND YOUR POWER.

WHAT IS NEEDED

A great many think that we need new measures, new churches, new organs, new choirs, and all these new things. That is not what the Church of God needs today. It is the old power that the apostles had. If we have that in our churches, there will be new life.

I remember when in Chicago many were toiling in the work, and it seemed as though the car of salvation didn't move on, when a minister began to cry out from the very depths of his heart:

"Oh, God, put new ministers in every pulpit."

Next Monday I heard two or three men stand up and say, "We had a new minister last Sunday—the same old minister, but he had got new power," and I firmly believe that is what we want today all over America—new ministers in the pulpit and new people in the pews. We want people quickened by the Spirit of God.

MINISTERS NEED TO BE QUICKENED BY THE SPIRIT OF GOD TO GET THE POWER OF THE APOSTLES TO REACH A LOST WORLD.

$\mathscr{F}$OLLOWING THE $\mathscr{L}$AMB

A friend who lost all his children told me about being in an eastern country some time ago, and he saw a shepherd going down to a stream, and he wanted to get his flock across. He went into the water and called them by name, but they came to the bank and bleated, and were too afraid to follow. At last he went back, tightened his girdle about his loins, took up two little lambs, and put one inside his frock, and another inside his bosom. Then he started into the water, and the old sheep looked up to the shepherd instead of down into the water. They wanted to see their little ones. So he got them over the water, and led them into the green pasture on the other side.

How many times the Good Shepherd has come down here and taken a little lamb to the hilltops of glory, and then the father and mother begin to look up and follow.

◆••◆••◆••◆••◆••◆••◆••◆••◆••◆••◆••◆••◆••◆••◆••◆••◆

WHEN GOD TAKES OUR CHILDREN FROM US,
HE COMES BACK TO BRING US TO
THAT PLACE AS WELL.

FALSE IDEAS ABOUT REPENTANCE

The unconverted have a false idea about repentance; they think God is going to make them repent. I was once talking with a man on this subject, and he summed up his whole argument by saying:

"Moody, it has never struck me yet."

I said, "What has never struck you?"

"Well," he replied, "some people it strikes, and some it doesn't. There was a good deal of interest in our town a few years ago, and some of my neighbors were converted, but it didn't strike me."

That man thought that repentance was coming down someday to strike him like lightning. Another man said he expected some sensation, like cold chills down his back.

Repentance isn't feeling. It is turning from sin to God. One of the best definitions was given by a soldier. Someone asked him how he was converted. He said:

"The Lord said to me, *Halt! Attention! Right about face! March!* and that was all there was in it."

GOD CANNOT MAKE US REPENT—WE MUST CHANGE OUR WAYS AND OBEY HIM OURSELVES, DEPENDENT ON HIS GRACE.

PULL FOR THE SHORE

A vessel was wrecked off the shore. Eager eyes were watching and strong arms manned the lifeboat. For hours they tried to reach that vessel through the great breakers that raged and foamed on the sandbank, but it seemed impossible. The boat appeared to be leaving the crew to perish. But after a while the captain and sixteen men were taken off, and the vessel went down.

"When the lifeboat came to you," said a friend, "did you expect it had brought some tools to repair your old ship?"

"Oh, no," was the response, "she was a total wreck. Two of her masts were gone, and if we had stayed mending her only a few minutes, we must have gone down, sir."

"When once off the old wreck and safe in the lifeboat, what remained for you to do?"

"Nothing, sir, but just to pull for the shore."

Man can't save himself. He has been wrecked by sin, and his only safety lies in taking Jesus Christ as his Savior.

WE WILL MAKE A WRECK
OF OUR OWN LIFE IF WE DON'T
RUN TO THE SAFETY OF THE SAVIOR.

*S*PIRITUAL *M*ATURITY

When I was at Wellesley College the other day, a young lady said, "Is it true, Mr. Moody, as so many tell us, that these are the best days of our lives?" I said, "No, not if you are children of God walking with Him." I have served Christ for twenty-one years and this last year has been the best. It grows better and better. I mount up higher and higher every year. I have had more peace, more strength, more rest the past year, than I ever had in my life. When I was converted I thought I got a great boon, the greatest I had ever received. I wondered if it would seem as pleasant to me after a few years, and if these things would not come to be old things. But Christ is a thousand times more to me now than He was then. You know that some men grow smaller and smaller on an intimate acquaintance; but my experience is that the more and more you know of Christ the larger He becomes.

AS WE BECOME MORE ACQUAINTED
WITH THE SAVIOR, HE BECOMES
FAR MORE PRECIOUS TO US.

THE POWER OF DEDICATION

A young woman was about to go to China as the wife of a missionary. She had a large Sunday school class in the city and succeeded in being a blessing to many of her scholars. She was very anxious to get someone who would look after her little flock and take care of them while she was gone. She had a brother who was not a Christian, and her heart was set on his being converted and taking her place as leader of the class. The young man refused to accept Christ, but away in her closet alone she pleaded with God that her brother might be converted and take her place. She wanted to reproduce herself.

That is what every Christian ought to do—get somebody else converted to take up your work. Well, the last morning came, and around the family altar as the moment drew near for the lady's departure, and they did not know when they should see her again, the father broke down, and the boy went upstairs. Just before she left for the train the boy came down, and putting his arms around his sister's neck, said to her, "My dear sister, I will take your Savior for mine, and I will take care of your class for you." The young man took her class and learned God's truth while he taught it. The last I heard of him he was still filling her place. There was a young lady established in good work.

◆━◆━◆━◆━◆━◆━◆━◆━◆━◆━◆━◆━◆━◆━

IF OTHERS ARE CONVERTED THEY CAN CARRY
ON THE WORK THAT GOD HAD US START.

RELIGIOUS EDUCATION OF CHILDREN

One of Coleridge's friends once objected to prejudicing the minds of the young by selecting the things they should be taught. The philosopher-poet invited him to take a look at his garden, and took him to where a luxuriant growth of ugly and pungent weeds spread themselves over beds and walks alike. "You don't call that a garden!" said his friend. "What!" said Coleridge, "would you have me prejudice the ground in favor of roses and lilies?"

Have you never noticed the same thing about the mind and the heart? Let a child be idle, and Satan will soon lead him into mischief. He must be looked after. Those things that will help to develop character must be selected for him. Hurtful things must be kept out, just as industriously as the farmer cultivates the useful products of the soil, but wages continual war on weeds and all unwholesome growth.

◆••◆••◆••◆••◆••◆••◆••◆••◆••◆••◆••◆••◆•

FILL YOUR CHILD'S MIND AND HEART WITH THE GOOD THINGS OF GOD.

THE DANGER OF LAZINESS

I once read of the founder of the Russian Empire going down to a Dutch seaport as a stranger, in disguise, that he might learn how to build ships, that he might go back and teach it to his own subjects. People have wondered at that, but this is a greater wonder, that the Prince of Glory should come down here and learn the carpenter's trade. He was not only the son of a carpenter, but He was a carpenter Himself. And right here is one lesson that we ought to learn, and that is, when Christ was here He was an industrious man, and I have often said on this platform that I never knew yet a lazy man to be converted. If he was, he soon gave up his laziness.

I tell you, laziness does not belong to Christ's kingdom. I don't believe a man would have a lazy hair in his head if he was converted to the Lord Jesus Christ. If a man has really been born of the Spirit of Christ, he isn't lazy; he desires something to do. Let us be willing to go out and work. If we can't find what we want, let us do what we can find until something better comes our way. A good many people are always waiting for something to turn up, instead of going out and turning up something. Look for something and you will likely find it.

LAZINESS DOES NOT BELONG TO THOSE WHO SERVE GOD. GO OUT AND FIND SOMETHING; IT WON'T FIND YOU.

THE PILGRIM NATURE OF FAITH

I was going to New Orleans from Chicago a few years ago, and there were two ladies on the train near me. They got well acquainted with one another by the time they reached Cairo, Illinois, where one lived; the other was going on to New Orleans. The one who had to get out at Cairo said to the other, "I wish you would stay here with me for a few days, I like your company so much." "I should like to stay," replied the other, "but my things are all packed and have gone on before; I have no clothes but those I am wearing. They are good enough to travel in, but I would not like to be seen in company with them."

Now that is the way with the Christian. We are away from home here, our treasure has gone on before, and anything is good enough to travel in. If things don't go smoothly down here we need not be too particular, they're good enough to travel in. If our treasures are in heaven our hearts will be there, and we shall be living as pilgrims and strangers on the earth. That is what I think of the journey of this world. A very little is good enough for us to travel in. We are all travelers, and this is good enough for traveling. We have raiment and mansions up there, waiting for us. Let us have our hearts and affections set on things above, and not on things on the earth.

AS PILGRIMS WE DON'T NEED MUCH TO
TRAVEL WITH. OUR REAL TREASURES
ARE IN THE PLACE WE ARE GOING.

THE CONVERSION OF AN INFIDEL

When I was in Edinburgh at the inquiry meeting in Assembly Hall, one of the ushers came around and said, "Mr. Moody, I'd like to put that man out; he's one of the greatest infidels in Edinburgh." I went around to where he was and sat down by him. "How is it with you, my friend?" I asked, and then he laughed and said, "You say God answers prayer; I tell you He doesn't. I don't believe in God. Try it on me." "Will you get down with me and pray?" I asked him, but he wouldn't. So I got down on my knees beside him and prayed.

Next night he was there again. I prayed, and quite a number of others prayed for him. A few months after that, away up in the north of Scotland, at Wick, I was preaching in the open air, and while I stood there I saw the infidel standing on the outskirts of the crowd. I went up to him at the close of the meeting and said, "How is it with you, my friend?" He laughed and said, "I told you your praying is all false. God hasn't answered your prayers; go and talk to these deluded people."

Shortly after, I got a letter from an attorney who is a Christian. He was preaching one night in Edinburgh, when this infidel went up to him and said, "I want you to pray for me; I am troubled." The barrister asked, "What is the trouble?" He replied, "I don't know what's the matter, but I don't have any peace, and I want you to pray for me." Next day he went around to that lawyer's office, and he said that he had found Christ.

MANY WHO FIND GOD BEGIN BY ATTACKING HIM, BUT THE HOLY SPIRIT CONVICTS THEM.

THE OLD AND NEW CREATION

A friend of mine said that when he was converted and began preaching, he talked a good deal about himself. He said one day he saw in one of the hymnbooks left by a godly woman who had a seat in the church, a flyleaf on which was written these words: "Dear Harry: not I, but Christ; not flesh, but spirit; not sight, but faith." These words my friend pasted in his Bible, and never preached or thought anymore about himself. He kept himself out of the way. That is just what the old man does not do. With him it is self, self, self. If it is the new man, it is not I, *but Christ.*

If it is the new man, it is not flesh, but spirit. If it is the new man, it is not sight but faith. In the old Adam it is death; in the new Adam it is eternal life. We all come under the two heads. Which, my friend, do you belong to, the old creation or the new? Let us pray that we may stand by the throne of God clothed in the righteousness of the second Adam.

CHRIST IS OUR HEAD,

OUR GREAT SHEPHERD.

CONVERSION OF A SKEPTICAL WOMAN

When Mr. Sankey and I were in the north of England, I was preaching one evening, and before me sat a lady who was a skeptic. When I had finished, I asked all who were concerned about their souls to remain. Nearly all remained, herself among the number. I asked her if she was a Christian, and she said she was not, nor did she care to be. I prayed for her there. On inquiry, I learned that she was a lady of good social position, but very worldly. She continued to attend the meetings, and in a week after I saw her in tears. After the sermon, I went to her and asked if she was of the same mind as before. She replied that Christ had come to her and she was happy.

Last autumn I had a note from her husband saying she was dead, that her love for the Master had continually increased. When I read that note, I felt paid for crossing the Atlantic. She worked sweetly after her conversion, and was the means of winning many of her fashionable friends to Christ. Oh, may you seek the Lord while He may be found, and may you call upon Him while He is near.

THE CONVERSION OF JUST
ONE SINNER IS WORTH A TRIP TO
THE OTHER SIDE OF THE OCEAN.

SUBSTITUTIONARY ATONEMENT

When the California gold fever broke out, a man went there leaving his wife in New England with his boy. As soon as he was successful he was to send for them. It was a long time before he succeeded, but at last he got money enough to send for them. The wife's heart leaped for joy. She took her boy to New York, got on board a Pacific Steamer, and sailed away to San Francisco. They had not been long at sea before the cry of "Fire! Fire!" rang through the ship, and rapidly it gained on them. There was a powder magazine on board, and the captain knew the moment the fire reached the powder, every man, woman, and child must perish.

They got out the lifeboats, but they were too small! In a minute they were overcrowded. The last one was just pushing away, when the mother pled with them to take her and her boy. "No," they said, "we have got as many as we can hold." She entreated them so earnestly, that at last they said they would take one more. Do you think she leaped into that boat and left her boy to die? No! She seized her boy, gave him one last hug, kissed him, and dropped him over into the boat. "My boy," she said, "if you live to see your father, tell him that I died in your place."

That is a reminder of what Christ has done for us. He laid down His life for us.

CHRIST DIED IN OUR PLACE TO SAVE US
FROM DROWNING IN A SEA OF SIN.

THE MISUNDERSTANDING OF ASSURANCE

A poor old widow, living in the Scottish Highlands, was called upon one day by a gentleman who had heard that she was in need. The old lady complained of her condition and remarked that her son was in Australia and doing well. "But does he not help you?" inquired the visitor. "No, he does nothing," was the reply. "He writes me regularly once a month, but only sends me a little picture with his letter." The gentleman asked to see one of the pictures that she had received, and found each of them to be a draft for ten pounds. She was regularly receiving more than enough money to meet her needs and having never seen a pound note she did not realize what she had.

That is the condition of many of God's children. He has given us many "exceeding great and precious promises," which we either are ignorant of or fail to appropriate. Many of them seem to be pretty pictures of an ideal peace and rest, but are not appropriated as practical helps in daily life. And not one of these promises is more neglected than the assurance of salvation. An open Bible places them within reach of all, and we may appropriate the blessing which such a knowledge brings.

⟡

WE HAVE WONDERFUL PROMISES OF ASSURANCE OF SALVATION IF WE WILL ONLY DISCOVER AND BELIEVE THEM.

WEST AND LORD LYTTLETON

It is said of West, an eminent man, that he was going to take up the doctrine of the resurrection, and just show the world what a fraud it was, while Lord Lyttleton was going to take up the conversion of Saul, and just show the folly of it. These men were going to annihilate that doctrine and that incident of the gospel. A Frenchman said it took twelve fishermen to build up Christ's religion, but one Frenchman pulled it down. From Calvary this doctrine rolled along the stream of time, through the eighteen hundred years, down to us, and West got at it and began to look at the evidence. But instead of his being able to cope with it he found it perfectly overwhelming—the proof that Christ had risen, that He had come out of the sepulchre and ascended to heaven and led captivity captive. The light dawned upon him, and he became an expounder of the Word of God and a champion of Christianity. And Lord Lyttleton, that infidel and skeptic, hadn't been long at the conversion of Saul before the God of Saul broke upon his sight, and he too, began to preach.

SETTING OUT TO DESTROY THE DOCTRINE OF THE RESURRECTION CAN ACTUALLY MAKE YOU CONVINCED OF ITS TRUTH.

*L*OOKING *S*AVES

I once heard of a woman who was greatly troubled by her sins, and she never could find out what the matter was. Why? Because she was always looking within, and one night when she went to bed greatly troubled she had a dream, and she dreamt that she was down in a deep pit, and that she was trying to get out. She would step up and when she had nearly got up to the top she would slip back. And she would climb up again, and then she would slip back again. She tried and failed, and tried and failed, and she gave up all hope, and she lay down there to die. She looked up and saw a little star, and it seemed in the dream as if that little star lifted her up, and she kept her eye upon it. She was nearly out when she took her eyes off it and looked at herself, and then she went down again. The second time the same thing happened, but the third time she did not take her eyes off the star, and she soon was lifted up higher and higher, until she felt her feet upon the rocks above, and she saw that if she were to be saved she must look to the Star of Bethlehem. No minister can save you. Nothing in the world can save you. You cannot save yourself. There is no other way but through Jesus.

DON'T LOOK WITHIN, LOOK TO THE CROSS OF CHRIST.

THE LONDON CHAMBER OF HORROR

When I was in London I went into a wax work there—Tassands—and I went into the chamber of Horror. There were wax figures of all kinds of murderers in that room. There was Booth who killed Lincoln, and many of that class. But there was one figure I got interested in, who killed his wife because he loved another woman, and the law didn't find him out. He married this woman and had a family of seven children. And twenty years passed away. Then his conscience began to trouble him. He had no rest; he would hear his murdered wife pleading continually for her life. His friends began to think that he was going out of his mind. He became haggard and his conscience haunted him till, at last, he went to the officers of the law and told them that he was guilty of murder. He wanted to die, life was so much of an agony to him. His conscience turned against him. My friends if you have done wrong, may your conscience be woke up, and may you testify against yourself. It is a great deal better to judge our own acts and confess them, than go through this world with the curse upon us.

OUR GUILTY CONSCIENCES MAY
EVENTUALLY COMPEL US TO REPENT,
NO MATTER WHAT THE COST.

MR. MOODY'S LITTLE DAUGHTER

I remember one time my little girl was teasing her mother to get her a muff, and so one day her mother brought a muff home, and, although it was storming, she very naturally wanted to go out in order to try her new muff. So she tried to get me to go out with her.

I went out with her, and I said, "Emma, better let me take your hand." She wanted to keep her hands in her muff, and so she refused to take my hand. Well, by and by she came to an icy place, her little feet slipped, and down she went. When I helped her up she said, "Papa, you may give me your little finger."

"No, my daughter, just take my hand."

"No, no, Papa, give me your little finger."

Well, I gave my finger to her, and for a little way she got along nicely, but pretty soon we came to another icy place, and again she fell. This time she hurt herself a little, and she said, "Papa, give me your hand," and I gave her my hand, and closed my fingers about her wrist, and held her up so that she could not fall.

Just so God is our keeper. He is wiser than we.

GOD KNOWS HOW TO TAKE CARE OF US,
EVEN IN THE SMALL AREAS OF LIFE,
BETTER THAN WE CAN OURSELVES.

A Father's Love

One morning my daughter was as cross as ever, and when she came to me to be kissed before going to school, I wouldn't do it. Off she went to her mother, and said: "Mamma, Papa refused to kiss me. I cannot go to school because he won't kiss me." Her mother came in, but she didn't say much. She knew the child had been doing wrong.

The little one went off, and as she was going downstairs I heard her weeping, and it seemed to me as if that child was dearer to me than ever she had been before. I went to the window and saw her going down the street crying, and as I looked on her I couldn't repress my tears.

That seemed to be the longest day I ever spent in Chicago. Before the closing of the school I was at home, and when she came in her first words were: "Papa, won't you forgive me?" and I kissed her and she went away singing. It was because I loved her that I punished her.

My friends, don't let Satan make you believe when you have any trouble, that God does not love you.

GOD CHASTISES US BECAUSE HE LOVES US AND FORGIVES US WHEN WE REPENT.

"THE HUMBUG"

There was a little man, while we were in London, who got out a little paper called "The Moody and Sankey Humbug." He used to have it to sell to the people coming into the meeting. After he had sold a great many thousand copies of that number, he wanted to get out another number. So he came to the meeting to get something to put into the paper, but the power of the Lord was present.

It says in chapter 5 of Luke that the Pharisees, scribes, and doctors, were watching the words of Christ in that house in Capernaum, and that the power of the Lord was present to heal.

It doesn't say they were healed. They did not come to be healed. But sometimes there is a prayer of faith going up to God from someone who brings down blessings.

And so this man came into that meeting. The power of the Lord was present, and the arrow of conviction went down deep into his heart. He went out, not to write a paper, but to destroy his paper that he had written, and so to tell what the Holy Ghost had done for him.

THE PRAYER OF FAITH CAN BRING CONVERSION AND HEALING.

UNDER THE JUNIPER TREE

There is a large class of people who are always looking upon the dark side. Sometime ago I myself got under the juniper tree. In those days I used to fish all night and catch nothing. One of the workers in our Mission came in to see me one Monday morning, full of joy, saying what a good Sunday he had. "Well," said I, "I am glad you have had a good day, but I have had a very bad one." He knew I had been in trouble of mind and so he said, "Did you ever study Noah?" "No," said I, "I have read about him, but I don't know that I have ever studied him." "Well," said he, "study him. It will do you good." So I began to study Noah, and I found out that he preached for a hundred and twenty years without making a single convert. "That is a good deal worse than my case," thought I, and that made me feel better at once. That day I went down to the noon prayer meeting, and one poor sinner rose and asked us to pray for him. "What would old Noah have given for that?" thought I. I tell you, what we want is perseverance.

PATIENCE AND PERSEVERANCE ARE
BOTH NEEDED IN TERMS OF SEEING
GOD WORK IN THE LIVES OF SINNERS.

SELF-RIGHTEOUSNESS

An artist wanted a man who would represent the prodigal. One day, he met a poor beggar, and he thought— "That man would represent the prodigal." He found the beggar ready to sit for his painting if he would pay him. The man appeared on the day appointed, but the artist did not recognize him. He said, "You made an appointment with me." "No," says the artist, "I never saw you before." "You are mistaken; you did see me, and made an appointment with me." "No, it must be some other artist. I have an appointment to meet a beggar here at this hour." "Well," says the beggar, "I am the man." "You are the man?" "Yes." "What have you been doing?" "Well, I thought I would get a new suit of clothes before I got painted." "Well," says the artist, "I don't want you." He would not have him then. And so if you are coming to God, come just as you are. Do not go and put on some garments of yours, and think the Lord will accept you because you have some good thoughts and desires.

• • • • • • • • • • • • • • • • • • •

GOD WANTS US TO COME TO HIM JUST AS WE ARE, WITHOUT PRIDE OR PRETENSE.

GREAT REVIVAL

My boy, the Lord wants you. Seek ye first the kingdom of God, and seek Him while He may be found. About eighteen years ago, a great revival swept over America. A great many men stood and shook their heads; they could not believe it was a healthy state of things. The Church was not in its normal state! The Church from Maine to Minnesota, and on to California, was astir. As you passed over the great republic, over its western prairies and mountains, and through its valleys, as you went on by train, and as you passed through its cities and villages, you could see the churches lit up. Men were flocking into the kingdom of God by hundreds. And in a year and a half or two years there were more than half a million souls brought in. Men said it was false excitement, wildfire, and it would pass away. But, my friends, it was the grace preceding judgment. Little did we know that our nation was soon to be baptized in blood, and that we would soon hear the tramp of a million men, that hundreds and thousands of our young men, the flower of our nation, would soon be lying in soldiers' graves. But oh, my friends, it was God calling His people in. He was preparing our nation for a terrible struggle.

GOD USED REVIVAL TO PREPARE
THE NATION FOR THE CIVIL WAR.

*L*OST *E*YESIGHT

I was in an eye infirmary in Chicago some time ago, before the great fire. A mother brought a beautiful little babe to the doctor—a babe only a few months old—and wanted the doctor to look at the child's eyes. He did so and pronounced it blind—blind for life—it will never see again. The moment he said that, the mother seized the baby, pressed it to her bosom, and gave a terrible scream. It pierced my heart, and I could not but weep. What a fearful thought to that mother! "Oh, my darling," she cried, "are you never to see the mother that gave you birth?" It was a sight to move any heart. But what is the loss of eyesight to the loss of a soul? I would a thousand times rather have these eyes taken out of my head and go to the grave blind, than lose my soul. I have a son, and no one but God knows how I love him. But I would see those eyes dug out of his head tonight rather than see him grow up to manhood and go down to the grave without Christ and without hope. The loss of a soul! Christ knew what it meant. That is what brought Him from the bosom of the Father; that is what brought Him from the throne; that is what brought Him to Calvary.

THOUGH WE UNDERGO MANY TRAGEDIES IN
LIFE, THE LOSS OF OUR IMMORTAL SOUL
IS FAR WORSE THAN ANY.

*T*ROUBLE *D*EVELOPS *L*OVE

When the despatch came that Chicago was burning up, that 100,000 people were turned out of house and home, then everyone became so interested that they began to weep for us. They came forward and laid down their money—some gave hundreds of pounds—for the relief of the poor sufferers. It was the *calamity* of Chicago that brought out the love of Manchester, and of London, and of Liverpool. I was in that terrible fire, and I saw men who were wealthy stripped of all they had. That Sunday night, when they retired, they were the richest men in Chicago, next morning they were paupers. But I did not see a man weep. When the news came flashing along the wire, "Liverpool is giving a thousand pounds; Manchester is giving a thousand pounds; London is giving money to aid the city;" and as the news kept flashing that help was coming, that city was brokenhearted. I saw men weep then. The love that was showed us, that love broke our hearts. So the love of God ought to break every heart in this city. It was love that brought Christ down here to die for us. It was love that made Him leave His place by the Father's throne and come down here *to seek and to save that which was lost.*

THE LOVE OF GOD SHOULD BREAK OUR HEARTS BECAUSE OF ITS INTENSITY AND FULLNESS.

*W*ORLDLY *W*ISDOM

*S*uppose I should say I lost a very valuable diamond here last night—I have not, but suppose it—worth £20,000. I had it in my pocket when I came into the hall, and when I had done preaching I found it was not in my pocket, but was in the hall somewhere. And suppose I was to say that anyone who found it could have it. How earnest you would all become! You would not get very much of my sermon; you would all be thinking of the diamond. I do not believe the police could get you out of this hall. The idea of finding a diamond worth £20,000! If you could only find it, it would lift you out of poverty at once, and you would be independent for the rest of your days. Oh, how soon everybody would become terribly in earnest then! I would to God I could get men to seek for Christ in the same way. I have got something worth more than a diamond to offer you. Is not salvation—eternal life—worth more than all the diamonds in the world? Suppose Gabriel should wing his way from the throne of God and come down here, and say he had been commissioned by Jehovah to come and offer to this assembly any one gift you might choose. You could have just what you chose, but only one thing. What would it be? The wealth of England or of the world? Would that be your choice? Ten thousand times, no! Your one cry would be, "Life! Eternal life!"

SALVATION IS WORTH MORE THAN THE MOST PRICELESS POSSESSIONS OF EARTH.

CONVERSION OF CHILDREN

*T*he mother was dead, and little Nellie, ten years old, wanted to follow in her footsteps. The father said yes, and she led them off to the chamber to pray. When they came out he noticed that they had been weeping, and asked what about. "Well, father," said the little girl, "I prayed just as Mother taught me, and then"—naming her little brother— "he prayed the prayer that Mother taught him; but little Susie, she was too young, Mother had not taught her a prayer, so she made a prayer of her own, and I could not help but weep to hear her pray." "Why," said the father, "what did she say?" "Why, she put up her little hands, and closed her eyes, and said, 'O God, You have come and taken away my dear Mamma, and I have no Mamma to pray for me now—won't You please make me good just as my dear Mamma was, for Jesus' sake, Amen.'" God heard that prayer. That little child before she was four years old gave evidence of being a child of God, and for sixteen years she was in that heathen country leading little children to the Lamb of God that taketh away the sin of the world.

OUT OF THE MOUTHS OF BABES
COMES PROFOUND TRUTH.

CHRIST AND HYPOCRITES

Some people say, "I have no doubt about the Word of God, but there are some men in the church who ought not to be there; therefore, I do not purpose to go into the church." I am not asking you to come into the church—not but what I believe in churches, but I am asking you to the marriage supper of the Lamb. But you say, here are some hypocrites. "Here is a man up here in one of the churches who cheated me out of £5 a few years ago, and you are not going to catch me in the company of hypocrites." Well, my friend, if you want to get out of the company of hypocrites, you had better get out of the world as quick as you can. One of the twelve apostles turned out to be a hypocrite, and there is no doubt there will be hypocrites in the church to the end of time. But "what is that to thee?" says Christ to Peter, "follow thou Me." We do not ask you to follow hypocrites, we ask you to follow Christ. We do not ask you to believe in hypocrites, we ask you to believe in Christ. Another thing, if you want to get out of the company of hypocrites you had better make haste and come to Christ. There will be no hypocrites at the marriage supper of the Lamb. They will all be in hell, and you will be there with them if you do not make haste and come to Christ.

•─•••─•••─•••─•••─•••─•••─•••─•••─•••─•••─•

**HYPOCRITES HAVE NO PLACE
IN GOD'S KINGDOM, SO FORSAKE
THIS DETESTABLE PRACTICE.**

FAITH, NOT REASON

I heard of some commercial travelers who went to hear a man preach. They came back to the hotel, and were sitting in the smoking room. They said the minister did not appeal to their reason, and they would not believe anything they could not reason out. An old man sitting there listening, said to them, "You say you won't believe anything you can't reason out?" "No, we won't." The old man said, "As I was coming on the train I noticed some sheep and cattle and swine and geese, eating grass. Now, can you tell me by what process that same grass was turned into feathers, hair, bristles, and wool?" "Well, no, we can't just tell you that." "Do you believe it is a fact?" "Oh, yes, it is a fact." "I thought you said you would not believe anything you could not reason out?" "Well, we can't help believing that; we see it with our eyes." "Well," said the old man, "I can't help but believe in regeneration, and a man being converted, although I cannot explain how God converted him."

WE CANNOT REASON OUT THE PROCESS
OF SALVATION, BUT MANY FACTS
CANNOT BE REASONED ANYWAY.

No Time!

*I*s it true you have no time? What did you do with the 365 days of last year? Had you no time during all these twelve months to seek the kingdom of God? You spend *twenty years* getting an education to enable you to earn a living for this poor frail body, so soon to be eaten up of worms. You spend *seven or eight years* in learning a trade that you may earn your daily bread; and yet you have not *five minutes* to accept of this invitation of Christ's! My friend, bear in mind you have yet to find time to die, to stand in the presence of the Judge. And when He calls you to stand before that bar, will you dare to tell Him that you had no time to prepare for the marriage supper of His Son? You have no time? Take time! Let everything else be laid aside until you have accepted this invitation. Do you not know that it is a lie? If you have not time, take it. "Seek *first* the kingdom of God." Let the children sit up a little late tonight. Let your business be suspended tomorrow. Suppose you do not get so much money tomorrow. What matter it if you get Christ? Better for a man to be sure of salvation than to "gain the whole world and lose his own soul."

REALIZE HOW MUCH TIME YOU SPEND ON UNIMPORTANT THINGS AND THEN GIVE GOD THE BEST YOU HAVE.

THE FATHER'S WILL

I remember a story of a bad boy who ran away from home. He had refused all the invitations which his father had sent him to come home and be forgiven, and help to comfort his old heart. He had even gone so far as to scoff at his father and mother. But one day a letter came telling him his father was dead, and they wanted him to come home and attend the funeral. At first he would not go, but then he thought it would be a shame not to pay some little respect to the memory of so good a man after he was dead. And so, just as a matter of form, he took the train, and went to the old home, sat through all the funeral services, saw his father buried, and came back with the rest of the friends to the house, with his heart as cold and stony as ever. But when the old man's will was brought out, the ungrateful son found that his father had remembered him in the will, and had left him an inheritance with the others, who had not gone astray. This broke his heart. That is just the way our Father in heaven does with sinners. He loves them in spite of their sins, and it is the love which, more than anything else, brings hard-hearted sinners to their knees.

* * *

GOD CONTINUES TO LOVE US IN SPITE
OF OUR SINS AND HAS HIS WAY
OF BRINGING US INTO SUBMISSION.

*F*REE

*I*n the British Colonies, before the time of Wilberforce, there used to be a great many slaves. That good man began to agitate the question of setting them free, and all the slaves in the colonies were anxious to know how he was getting along. But in those days there were no telegraphs and no steamships. The mail went by the slow sailing vessels. They would be from six to eight months in making a voyage to some of the colonies. The slaves used to watch for the British ships, hoping to hear good news, but fearing they might hear bad news. There was a ship which had sailed immediately after the Emancipation Act had been passed and signed by the king. And when she came within hailing distance of the boats which had put off from the shore at the port where she was bound, the captain could not wait to deliver the message officially, and have it duly promulgated by the government. But, seeing the poor, anxious men standing up in their boats, eager for the news, he placed his trumpet to his mouth, and shouted with all his might, "Free! Free!" Just so the angels shout when a poor bondman is taken in hand by the Savior Himself, delivered from the bondage of darkness into the liberty of His dear Son. Free—free from sin—free from the curse of the law.

HOW WONDERFUL IT IS TO BE DELIVERED FROM THE BONDAGE OF OUR SIN INTO THE GLORIOUS FREEDOM OF GOD'S CHILDREN.

CHEERFULNESS—AN ATTRACTION OF PIETY

A London minister lately pointed out a family of seven, all of whom he was just receiving into the church. Their story was this: Going to church, he had to pass by a window, looking up at which one day he saw a baby looking out. He smiled—the baby smiled. Next time he passes he looks up again, smiles, and the baby smiles back. A third time going by, he looks up, and seeing the baby, throws it a kiss—which the baby returns to him. Time after time he has to pass the window, and now cannot refrain from looking up each time. And each time there are more faces to receive his smiling greeting, till by and by he sees the whole family grouped at the window—father, mother, and all. The father conjectures the happy, smiling stranger must be a minister, and so, next Sunday morning, after they have received at the window the usual greeting, two of the children, ready dressed, are sent out to follow him. They enter his church, hear him preach, and carry back to their parents the report that they never heard such preaching. Soon the rest come to the church, too, and are brought in—all by a smile. Let us not go about hanging our heads like a bulrush. If Christ gives us joy, let us live it!

A SMILE OF JOY CAN HAVE
A VERY POSITIVE EFFECT ON OTHERS.

*O*BEDIENCE

I remember reading in some history of the ninth century of a young general who with only five hundred men came up against a king with twenty thousand. And the king sent to him to say that it was the height of folly to resist with his handful of men. The general called in one of his men and said, "Take that sword and drive it into your heart." And the man took the weapon, and drove it into his heart, and fell dead. He said to another, "Leap into yonder chasm," and the man instantly obeyed. Then, turning to the messenger, he said, "Go back and tell your king that we have five hundred such men. We will die but we will never surrender." The messenger returned, and his tale struck terror into the hearts of the king's soldiers, so that they fled like chaff before the wind. God says, "One shall chase a thousand, and two shall put ten thousand to flight."

A STRONG AND VALIANT SOLDIER FOR
CHRIST CAN TAKE ON ANY CHALLENGE,
EVEN IF SEEMINGLY OUTNUMBERED.

THE BANNER OF THE CROSS

The Spanish authorities in Cuba had arrested a man who, though born in England, was a naturalized United States citizen. He was charged with conspiracy against the government, and ordered to be shot. But the consuls of both England and America believed the man to be innocent, and used all the persuasion and entreaty in their power for his release, but the proud Spaniards haughtily disregarded their petition.

The hour of execution had now arrived, and a company of soldiers were drawn up in line. The condemned English-American marched out before them, calmly awaiting his fate. He stood at the foot of the grave, already dug, his coat off, and his hands pinioned behind him. The officer ordered his men to load, and at the word "present," they brought their rifles to their shoulders, awaiting the word of command to fire.

In the awful suspense, suddenly there sprang forward from the bystanders the two consuls; the one drawing from his breast the Stars and Stripes, wrapping it right around the prisoner, whilst the other threw over him the Union Jack. The consuls now stood on either side, defying the Spaniards, who dared not fire on the flags of two of the mightiest nations under heaven. The man was released, and proved his innocence to the satisfaction of the authorities. Oh! To be wrapped in the blood-stained banner of the cross.

•─••─••─•─••─••─•─••─••─•─••─••─•─••─•

LET US WRAP OURSELVES IN THE BANNER OF CHRIST WHERE WE ARE TRULY SAFE.

A Love Feast Story

One Thanksgiving in our mission school I had appointed a kind of love feast, at which everyone was to tell what he was most thankful for.

One little fellow, who had no other relative in the world but a decrepit old grandfather, with whom he lived in the greatest poverty, had become a Christian some time before, and, like others of the children, was trying to do a little home-missionary work on his own account. When his turn came to tell what he was most thankful for, he said—

"There was that big fellow, 'Butcher Kilroy,' who acted so bad that nobody would have him, and he had to be turned out of one class after another, till I was afraid he would be turned out of the school. It took me a long time to get him to come, and I begged for him to stay. I used to pray to Jesus every day to give him a new heart, and I felt pretty sure He would if we didn't turn him out. By and by Butcher Kilroy began to want to be a Christian, and now he is converted. That is what makes this Thanksgiving the happiest one in all my life."

WE CAN BE THANKFUL THAT THE GREATEST
GIFT OF ALL IS THE PRESENCE
OF GOD IN OUR HEARTS.

A Western Judge

Special prayer was offered for him at the Fulton street prayer meeting and other places. Sometime afterward, when I returned to town, I met the judge, who told me of his conversion. One night his wife went to prayer meeting and during her absence he began to think, "Suppose my wife is right, that there is a hell and a heaven, and that my children are going to heaven and I am not." Conviction seized him and he commenced to pray. He retired before his wife returned and pretended to be asleep while she prayed for him. Rising early in the morning he told her he did not feel very well, and without waiting for breakfast, proceeded to his office. He told his clerks they might have a holiday, and shutting himself up in the office prayed that God for Christ's sake would take away the great load of guilt, and soon the burden rolled off. He told his wife that he was a new man, and they both knelt in prayer, thanking God for His great goodness. Upon returning to America I inquired if the judge stood firm. I was informed that he had passed gloriously from earth and was now standing at the right hand of God.

—————————

GOD IS FAITHFUL TO WAIT FOR THE BEST TIME TO REACH OUR HEARTS WITH HIS TRUTH, NO MATTER HOW RESISTANT.

Believe, Then Work

We work because we are saved. We do not work to be saved. We work from the cross and not toward it. I imagine some of you say, "Why does Paul say, then, 'Work out your own salvation with fear and trembling'?" You must have salvation before you can work it out. I must give my boy a garden before he can work the weeds out of it. If I said to him, "Be careful how you spend that hundred dollars," he would say, "give it to me first." When I first went to Boston my money was soon gone, and I was getting desperate. Although there was but one mail a day I went three times a day to the post office to see if I could get a letter from home. At last I got a letter, and it was from my little sister. She had heard there were pickpockets in Boston, and the burden of her letter was to have me be careful and not get my pocket picked. But I would have had to have money in my pocket before it could be picked. So you must have salvation before you can work it out.

•━•━•━•━•━•━•━•━•━•━•━•━•━•━•━•

OUR SALVATION IS SECURE, SO
LET US WORK HARD TO DO
THE WILL OF HIM WHO SENT US.

DUTY

*S*uppose I said to my wife that I loved her because it was my duty to love her, and suppose I should go to Connecticut to visit my aged mother, and suppose I should say to her, "Mother, you have been very good to me, and you are getting old now. You are on your way to the grave, you are living on borrowed time, and I feel it is my duty to come every year and see you." I think she would say, "My boy, you need not come anymore, if you come out of duty." Yet how many talk about duty to God? Let us strike for a higher plane, and work for Him *because we love Him.*

People are always trying to do some great thing for the Lord. They have no opportunity because they have no great thing to do. I once heard of a man who had a dream. He said that he was taken, as he died, by the angels to a beautiful temple built up with polished stones, but there was just one little stone left out. He asked the angel how it was. "The master builder," replied the angel, "intended that for you, but you wanted to build in some greater place." When he awoke he determined ever since that he would do anything to get in. He went right to work, and the Lord blessed him.

OUR LOVE FOR GOD IS NOT MERELY
A DUTY BUT A JOY, SO LET US SERVE
HIM WITH ALL OUR HEARTS.

A Good While Coming

While the yellow fever was raging in a Southern city, the father of a poor family who were strangers there was struck with the disease. It raged so fearfully that the city authorities had them buried the moment they died. The father was buried and the mother was stricken down. She knew that she soon would be gone, so she called her little boy and said, "When I am gone Jesus will come and take care of you." She had no one else to commend him to. The little boy followed her to the burial place, and then came home. It was night, and dark and dreary, and he got scared. He went up to the grave without his supper and lay down and slept till morning, when he got up cold and stiff. While he was on the grave weeping a stranger passed through and asked him what he was doing there. He said he was waiting for Jesus. "What do you mean, my boy?" said the man. The child told his story. God touched the man's heart, and he said, "Well, my boy, Jesus has sent me." "Well," said the little boy through his tears, "you have been a good while coming." Mr. Moody hoped, in conclusion, that anxious souls would not have the same complaint to make against the Christians who were present.

ALLOW GOD TO SEND YOU WHERE
THE GREATEST NEED IS, YOU MAY BE
THE ONLY [ONE] TO MAKE A DIFFERENCE.

*W*ATERLOGGED *C*HRISTIANS

A friend of mine said that he was in Liverpool sometime ago, and there was a vessel coming into the harbor. It sailed right up the Mersey under full sail, and a little while after another vessel came in towed by a tug and sunken to the level of the water. He wondered it did not sink, and he went down to the water's edge and saw why that they got it into the harbor with a great deal of difficulty, and he inquired and found that it was loaded with lumber. It had such material on board that it could not sink, and it had sprung a leak and had got waterlogged. My friends, I think there are a good many of God's people who have gotten waterlogged, and it takes all the strength of the church to look after those Christians. They are so waterlogged that they cannot go forth and do good to others—help the unfortunate, and lift up the poor drunkard. The fact is, they are off with the world, mingling with the world, acting and speaking as though in the world, and they don't know whether they are saved themselves.

LET US NOT BE LADEN DOWN
WITH WORLDLINESS OR WE
WILL NOT BE EFFECTIVE.

LIVING WATER

"Out of his belly shall flow rivers of living water."
That is the kind of Christian we ought to be.

When I was a boy I used to have to pump water for the cattle. Ah, how many times I have pumped with that old right hand until it ached, and many times I used to pump when I could not get any water. I was taught that when the pump was dry I must pour a pail of water down the pump and then I could get the water up.

And that is what Christians want—a well of living water. We will have plenty of grace to spare—all we need ourselves and plenty for others. We have got into the way now of digging artesian wells better. They don't pump now to get the water, but when they dig the well they cut down through the gravel and through the clay perhaps 1,000 or 2,000 feet, not stopping when they can pump the water up, but they cut to a lower strata and the water flows up abundantly of itself.

And so we ought every one of us to be like artesian wells. God has grace enough for every one of us.

LET GOD'S GRACE FLOW THROUGH YOU TO BLESS THE WORLD AROUND YOU.

THE CHRISTIAN BATTLE

It is said of Napoleon, after his army had gained a great victory, he was so pleased that he got a medal struck off, on one side of which was the date, and on the other these words, "I was through it all."

It is said of these old veterans that long years after they would bring out these medals and show them, and as they would tell of the battle their faces would light up and they would say, "I was there."

My friends, a great battle is now going on between the kingdom of heaven and the powers of darkness, and God wants all of us to do what we can. And by and by up yonder we shall talk of the battle we fought in this dark world, and be joyful to say, "I was there."

One thing has cheered us up beyond measure, and that is the spirit of unity we have seen. We have not heard a word about denominations since we have been to work in three of the great cities of our country. We have not heard one word about sect or party. Thanks be to God, we are just bound up in one bundle, and the moment we are a little more brought together in this way, Christianity will be like a red-hot ball rolling over the world.

REMEMBER, A GREAT BATTLE IS NOW GOING ON BETWEEN THE KINGDOM OF HEAVEN AND THE POWERS OF DARKNESS.

*P*ERSONAL *E*FFORT

I remember when in London a friend asked me to go down to the dog market and preach. It is a part of the city where men come to sell dogs and cats and birds. They had fighting-cocks there, and were trying to get up a fight. The streets were literally crowded with this class of men, but traffic went right on.

My friend said he wanted someone to preach who could get the attention of these men; and he thought if I would go, being an American, I might succeed. Some of them stopped a little while to listen, but I did not get into sympathy with them. One man came up to me with a fighting-cock, but I did not succeed in getting any hold on him. One of them, who had been converted a short time before, stood up on a chair and immediately all traffic stopped, a crowd gathered round to hear him, and this man in fifteen minutes did more than all of us put together.

❖◦━◦❖◦━◦❖◦━◦❖◦━◦❖◦━◦❖◦━◦❖◦━◦❖◦━◦❖

BE OBEDIENT TO TELL YOUR FRIENDS
AND FAMILY OF HIS WONDERFUL LOVE.

DR. DUFF

*I*n 1867, before I went to Europe, my friend Mr. Stuart of Philadelphia, said to me, "Be sure to be at the General Assembly at Edinburgh. I was there last year, and it did me a world of good." He said Dr. Duff was invited to speak to the General Assembly on the wants of India. After an hour and a half's urging on the importance of sending young men to India, the old man fainted away and was carried out. By and by he came to and wondered where he was. "I was making a plea for India," said he, "but I did not finish my speech. Take me back and let me finish it."

The physicians tried to stop him, but he said he would speak or die in the attempt. Mr. Stuart said it was one of the grandest sights he ever saw in his life. The whole congregation stood and the tears rolled down many cheeks while the old man with a trembling voice said, "Fathers and mothers of Scotland, is it true that you will not let your sons and your daughters go to India to preach the gospel? I spent twenty-five years of my life there, and lost my health, and have come back to die in Scotland. If it is true, I will pack up what few things I have and will be off tomorrow. I will let these heathen know if I cannot live for them I am willing to die for them."

The world will say that old man was enthusiastic, but that is just what we want. I suppose they said it of the Son of God.

PRAY TO SEND LABORERS INTO
THE HARVEST TO EXPAND THE KINGDOM.

CHRIST'S GUEST CHAMBER

Oh, what a sweet thought to think that we shall be forever with the Lord and that there will be no death there to come and mar the scene, that we shall be there with our loved ones and with the Lord, and shall behold Him forever. If a man dies in Christ this body shall be raised incorruptible, and we shall get a better body from which all death and imperfections shall be taken away. There is nothing there, my friends, that shall mar our happiness. A few more rolling years at the longest, and we shall be landed on Canaan's shore. But we must be faithful the few days we have here; it will not be long when all of us will be called away and our earthly conflict will be over. I would ask all here if you have an interest in Christ, if you have been buried and risen with Him, if your names are written in the Lamb's book of life.

You know I travel a good deal. When I come to the house of a friend he will take me to the guest chamber, where I shall find everything I need, perhaps even a bouquet of flowers. In fact, my friend anticipates all I want. So when Christ gets us into the guest chamber there will be nothing wanting.

LET US FIX OUR EYES ON JESUS.

*P*ILATE

*T*o me there rises up one solemn thought, all these men who would not decide for Christ how punishment came on them! Judas went out and hung himself, and then Caiaphas the high priest who wanted to keep his position, was deposed the next year. Herod was driven soon after to exile and died a terrible death. And Pilate was in a little while recalled by the emperor, and thus lost the office he wanted to hold. He went off into exile, and we have it on good authority that he went and put an end to his own existence. What a sad mistake he made—how his name might have been handed down through the ages, how it might have been associated with Peter and James and John. He was thoroughly convinced he ought to decide in favor of Christ, but he had not the moral courage. He was lost—lost for time and eternity for the want of decision—and I believe in my soul there are more today in America being lost for the want of decision than any other one thing.

BE STRONG IN THE LORD AND IN
HIS MIGHTY POWER.

THE POWER OF CONSCIENCE

A minister in Cleveland went to visit a prisoner in the city jail. He was there awaiting his trial. He was accused of murder, but few believed that he was guilty.

In the cell he confessed to the minister that he had done the deed. His friends said it was impossible. He could not have done it. But the man explained how he did it. He said the reason that he made the confession was, "I wanted to get away from myself." That is it. He wanted to get away from the cry of his conscience.

How it is that men dare to sin, then laugh and mock at sin, with eternity opening up before them, is one of the greatest mysteries of the day.

The Bible talks about the mystery of godliness, but that men will trifle with sin, and mock and laugh at sin, is a greater mystery to me.

MAN'S CONSCIENCE CAN BE DECEIVED,

HARDENED, AND EVEN DEAD.

CHRISTIAN WORKERS WANTED

I am thinking it is well for us to have fair misunderstanding with you. We have come just to gather in the harvest.

Now, the first class we want is the ministers. I was cheered when I came here today, but it was not the vast audience that cheered me, it was not the great building. It was the presence of the ministers on this platform, who seized me by the hand and gave me a "God bless you." It gave me a light heart. There are some ministers who get behind the posts, as if they were ashamed of being seen here at these meetings, but come to criticize the sermon and pick it to pieces. Anyone can criticize, it doesn't take brain or head to do it. Oh, if the ministers were of one spirit now a flame of fire would rise up in Chicago which would spread out into the country and through all the Northwest.

The next class we want to help us is the Sunday school teachers. What they want is a quickening to bring the children under their charge to Christ. Let every teacher in Chicago say, "By the help of God I will try and lead my class to Christ this season."

◆━━━━━━━━━━━━━◆

ALWAYS KEEP ON PRAYING FOR ALL THE SAINTS.

THE OBSTACLE OF UNBELIEF

The first stone you have got to roll away is unbelief. Now I would ask the Christian people of Chicago, do you believe God can revive His work here? Everyone would say, "Yes, I believe He can." What we want is to believe that He will do it. There is not an infidel in this city but knows God can do it.

I remember when we left Edinburgh and went to Glasgow the infidels said it had been a work among women and children, that no men were reached, none but the weak-minded.

We went to Glasgow, and we there made it a subject of prayer that we should reach the young men. The result was that out of 3,300 that made profession of Christianity there were over 1,700 men. It was then said, "Oh, they are almost all young men religiously brought up. The drunkards and the gamblers and hard cases are not reached." We made this also a subject of prayer. The next place we went the first convert was a gambler, and the second the most notorious drunkard in the place, and, thank God, these men hold out.

Now all through these years this sin of unbelief is the mother of all sin. May God strip it from us, and we shall have faith to believe that God will do a great work.

-·-•-··-•-··-•-··-•-··-•-··-•-··-•-·-

MAY GOD STRENGTHEN OUR FAITH IN ALL HIS PROMISES.

Up and *About It*

There was a mother in London who constantly prayed for her boy.

He at last said, "Mother, I am not going to be bothered by your prayers any longer. I am going to America."

Said she, "Your mother's prayers can reach you there; you will find that God is on the sea and in America."

He left there and came to this country. When he got to New York harbor someone told him we were holding meetings in the Hippodrome. When he got on shore he found that God was waiting for him. He became a Christian, and is now one of the best workers in New York City.

Before he went to bed he sat down and wrote to that mother that he had found the Savior.

If, mothers, you are going to work for God, you must be up and about it. Take time. Give fifteen or twenty minutes a day to God. You don't know what the result may be.

GIVE GOD TIME, SEEK HIM FIRST, AND
HE WILL ADD ALL OTHER THINGS UNTO YOU.

THE HOPE OF HEAVEN

What has been, and is now, one of the strongest feelings in the human heart? Is it not to find some better place, some lovelier spot, than we have now? It is for this that men are seeking everywhere. And yet, they can have it, if they will, but instead of looking down, they must look up to find it. As men grow in knowledge, they vie with each other more and more to make their homes attractive, but the brightest home on earth is but an empty barn, compared with the mansions that are in the skies.

What is it that we look for at the decline and close of life? Is it not some sheltered place, some quiet spot, where if we cannot have constant rest, we may at least have a foretaste of what is to be? What was it that led Columbus, not knowing what would be his fate, across the unsailed western seas, if it was not the hope of finding a better country? This it was that sustained the hearts of the Pilgrim fathers, driven from their native land by persecution, as they faced an ironbound, savage coast, with an unexplored territory beyond. They were cheered and upheld by the hope of reaching a free and fruitful country, where they could be at rest and worship God in peace.

Somewhat similar is the Christian's hope of heaven, only it is not an undiscovered country, and in attractions cannot be compared with anything we know on earth.

WE REJOICE IN THE HOPE OF THE GLORY OF HEAVEN.

*W*ITNESSING TO *P*ROSTITUTES

I remember when we were in England ten years ago, there was a woman in the city where we labored who got stirred up to do what she could. She had been a nominal Christian for a good many years, but she had not thought that she had any particular mission in the world. I am afraid that is the condition of many professed Christians.

This woman began to look about her to see what she could do. She thought she would try to do something for her fallen sisters in that city. She went out and began to talk kindly to prostitutes she met on the street. She rented a house and invited them to come and meet her there.

When we went back to that city about a year or so ago, she had rescued over three hundred of these fallen ones, and had restored them to their parents and homes. She is now corresponding with many of them. She did what she could. How she will rejoice when she hears the Master say, "Well done, good and faithful servant."

LET US SEEK TO KNOW OUR PURPOSE HERE ON EARTH AND FULFILL IT.

THE REDEMPTION BY CHRIST

A friend of mine once told me that he was going from Dublin one day, and met a boy who had one of those English sparrows in his hand. It was frightened, and just seemed to sit as if it pined for liberty, but the boy held it so tight that it could not get away. The boy's strength was too much for the bird.

My friend said, "Open your hand and let the bird go. You will never tame him, he is wild." But the boy replied, "Faith and I'll not; I've been a whole hour trying to catch him, an' now I've got him, I'm going to keep him."

So the man took out his purse and asked the boy if he would sell it. A bargain was made, and the sparrow was transferred to the man's hand. He opened his hand, and at first it did not seem to realize it had liberty, but by and by it flew away, and as it went it chirped, as much to say, "You have redeemed me." And so Christ has come down and offered to redeem us and give us liberty when we were bound with sin.

●━●━●━●━●━●━●━●━●━●━●━●━●━●━●━●━●━●━●

CHRIST HAS SET US FREE FROM GOD'S WRATH.

THE IMPORTANCE OF THE HOLY SPIRIT

When I first went to Scotland I was a little troubled about my theology for fear it wouldn't jibe with theirs. I hadn't my forehead covered with brass then. At one of the early meetings I saw one man with his head covered with his hands, and I thought he was mortified about my theology. When the meeting was over he grabbed his hat and away he went.

I gave him up and thought he wouldn't come again. He was absent the next few days, but one day he came to the prayer meeting, and there was such a change in him that I scarcely knew him. He said he was so thoroughly convinced that what I had said about the importance of being filled with the Holy Spirit was true that he felt he had been preaching without the power.

He had made up his mind to get it. So he locked himself in his closet, and God revealed Himself to his soul. It was not a month before the people couldn't get into that man's church it was so full of people. I met him before I sailed for this country, and he told me that he hadn't preached a sermon since without someone being converted.

LORD, FORGIVE US FOR UNDERESTIMATING THE POWER OF THE HOLY SPIRIT.

DISCIPLINE BASED ON LOVE

*I*n the little country district where I went to school there were two parties. One party said that boys could not possibly be controlled without the cane, and they kept a schoolmaster who acted on their plan. The other party said they should be controlled by love. The struggle went on, and at last, on one election day, the first party was put out, and the other ruled in their stead. I happened to be at the school at that time, and we said to each other that we were going to have a grand time that winter. There would be no more corporal punishment, and we were going to be ruled by love.

The new teacher was a lady, and she opened the school with prayer. We hadn't seen it done before, and we were impressed, especially when she prayed that she might have grace and strength to rule the school with love. The school went on for several weeks, and we saw no cane. I was one of the first to break the rules of the school. The teacher asked me to stay behind. I thought the cane was coming out again, and I was in a fighting mood. She sat down and began to talk to me kindly. That was worse than the cane; I did not like it. She said, "I have made up my mind that if I cannot control the school by love, I will give it up. I will have no punishment. If you love me, try to keep the rules of the school."

I felt something right here in my throat, and never gave her any more trouble. She just put me under grace. And that is what God does. God is love, and He wants us all to love Him. God wants us to obey Him in response to His love.

--- ◆ -- ◆ -- ◆ -- ◆ -- ◆ -- ◆ -- ◆ -- ◆ -- ◆ -- ◆ -- ◆ ---

LOVE ALWAYS TRUSTS, ALWAYS HOPES, ALWAYS PERSEVERES.

Culture is Inadequate to Regenerate

Culture is all right in its place, but culture won't regenerate a human heart. Suppose I commence the first day of May and plow an acre of ground crosswise, and the next day I plow it lengthwise, and every day in the week except Sunday I plow that acre of land. I begin the first day of May and plow all through May and June and July. Once in a while I put a cultivator in and cultivate it, and I harrow it, and brush it, and roll it.

I have been harrowing, brushing, rolling, and cultivating for months, and you come along and say, "Moody, what are you doing?" "Doing! I am cultivating this acre of land." "Well, I should say so! I was around here last May, and you were plowing that acre of land. Been at it ever since?" "Yes." "What were you going to put in it?" "Well, I am not going to put anything in it, but I believe in a high state of culture."

You would say I was a first-class lunatic! But that is what is going on all the while in spiritual things. Put the seed in, and then pray God that the dew of heaven may rest upon it, and you will have some results. There isn't a sower who goes forth and sows that kind of seed, but there are results.

◆━■━◆━■━◆━■━◆━■━◆━■━◆━■━◆━■━◆

LET THE WORD OF GOD DWELL IN YOU
RICHLY AND YOU WILL BEAR MUCH FRUIT.

PERSISTENCE IN WITNESSING

God uses the weak things of this world to confound the mighty. God's promise is better than a bank note—"I promise to pay so-and-so"—and here is one of Christ's promissory notes, "If you follow Me, I will make you fishers of men." Will you not lay hold of the promise, and trust it, and follow Him now? If we present the gospel, and present it faithfully, we ought to expect results then and there. I believe it is the privilege of God's children to reap the fruit of their labor 365 days of the year.

"Well, but," say some, "is there not a sowing time as well as a harvest?" Yes, it is true, there is; but then, you can sow with one hand and reap with the other. What would you think of a farmer who went on sowing all the year round and never thought of reaping? I repeat it, we want to sow with one hand and reap with the other; and if we look for the fruit of our labors, we shall see it. "I, if I be lifted up, will draw all men unto Me." We must lift Christ up and then seek men out and bring them to Him.

◆━◆━◆━◆━◆━◆━◆━◆━◆━◆━◆━◆━◆━◆

MAY WE BE FAITHFUL FOLLOWERS AND BOLD WITNESSES FOR JESUS' NAME'S SAKE.

TRUE RICHES

The Rev. John Newton one day called to visit a Christian family who had suffered the loss of all they possessed by fire. He found the wife and mother, and saluted her with, "I give you joy."

Surprised and ready to be offended, she exclaimed, "What! Joy that all my property is consumed?"

"Oh no," he answered, "but joy that you have so much property that fire cannot touch."

This allusion to her real treasures checked her grief and brought reconciliation. As it says in the fifteenth chapter of Proverbs: "In the house of the righteous is much treasure; but in the revenues of the wicked is trouble." I have never seen a dying saint who was rich in heavenly treasures who had any regret. I have never heard them say they had lived too much for God and heaven.

WHOSOEVER TRUSTS IN HIS RICHES WILL FAIL.

Do What You Can

The first two or three years that I attempted to talk in the meetings, I saw that the older people did not like it. I had sense enough to know that I was a bore to them. Well, I went out upon the street and I got eighteen little children to follow me the first Sunday, and I led them into the Sunday school. I found that I had something to do.

I was encouraged and I kept at that work. And if I am worth anything to the Christian church today, it is as much due to that work as anything else. I could not explain these scriptural passages to them for I did not then comprehend them, but I could tell them stories. I could tell them that Christ loved them and that He died for them. I did the best I could. I used the little talent I had, and God kept giving me more talents, and so, let me say, find some work.

See if you can get a Sunday school class to teach. If you cannot get that, go down into the dark lanes and byways of the city and talk to them and sing some gospel hymns, or, if you cannot sing, take someone with you who can sing some of these songs of praise.

LORD, ACCEPT OUR TALENTS AND
LET THEM GROW FOR YOU.

HONOR YOUR PARENTS

There was a very promising young man in my Sunday school in Chicago. His father was a confirmed drunkard, and his mother took in washing to educate her four children. This was her eldest son, and I thought that he was going to redeem the whole family.

But one day a thing happened that made him go down in my estimation. The boy was in the high school and was a very bright scholar. One day he stood with his mother at the cottage door—it was a poor house, but she could not pay for their schooling and feed and clothe her children and hire a very good house too out of her earnings.

When they were talking a young man from the high school came up the street, and this boy walked away from his mother. Next day the young man said, "Who was that I saw you talking to yesterday?" "Oh, that was my washer woman." I said, "Poor fellow! He will never amount to anything."

That was a good many years ago. I have kept my eye on him. He has gone down, down, down, and now he is just a miserable wreck. Of course, he would go down! Ashamed of his mother who loved him and toiled for him, and bore so much hardship for him! I cannot tell you the contempt I had for that one act.

HONOR YOUR FATHER AND YOUR MOTHER THAT IT MAY GO WELL WITH YOU.

THE JOY OF OBEDIENCE

Take the two Sauls. They lived about one thousand years apart. One started out well and ended poorly, and the other started out poorly and ended well. The first Saul got a kingdom and a crown; he had a lovely family (no father ever had a better son than Saul had in Jonathan); he had the friendship of Samuel, the best prophet there was on the face of the earth; and yet he lost the friendship of Samuel, lost his crown, his kingdom, his son, and his life, all through an act of disobedience.

Now take the Saul of the New Testament. When God called him, he was obedient to the heavenly vision, and he was given a heavenly kingdom. One act of obedience, one act of disobedience. The act of obedience gained all, and the act of disobedience lost everything. I believe the wretchedness and misery and woe in this country today come from disobedience to God. If people won't obey God as a nation, let us begin individually. Let us make up our minds that we will do it, cost us what it will, and we will have peace and joy.

TO PLEASE GOD YOU MUST FIRST OBEY HIM.

FORGIVENESS BEFORE SERVICE

When we were in Chicago there was a businessman who was going to take lunch with me. He came in late. I said, "How is this? I thought you were coming in right after the noon meeting." "Well," said he, naming another prominent businessman, "I had trouble with him six months ago, and I could not eat my lunch until I went down and asked his forgiveness." There was a good deal of that in Chicago, and that is one reason why I think the work was so great.

Let us have that in every community. If there is anybody that any of you ought to forgive, go and do it right away. I can imagine some of you saying, "They won't forgive me." But go to them and ask their forgiveness. I cannot make others forgive me, but I can forgive them. We must have nothing but love in our hearts. If they hate us and their hearts are filled with the fire of hell against us, we will forgive them in spite of that. We can love others whether they love us or not, and when we are right with God, He will speak through us and use us and not till then.

• — • — • — • — • — • — • — • — • — • — • — • — • — •

FORGIVE AND YOU SHALL BE FORGIVEN.

THE IMPORTANCE OF CHURCH

*L*et me speak to some of these new converts. I have heard it said that they're not going to unite themselves to any church. They think that they will sustain themselves outside of the church. They can't find a perfect church to go into. Now let me say that if you do not join a church until you find a perfect one, you will never find it. I have got done looking for a perfect church, a perfect minister, or a perfect anything upon earth. But there is nothing so dear to the Son of God as the church. Join one now and start working for your Lord.

A man told me that he would not stay here long, probably not more than a year or two, and it would not be worthwhile to join a church here. Well, can't you move your letter as easily as you can move your trunk? If I was going into fifty different towns I would carry a traveling letter, or take fifty letters. I would belong to fifty churches.

Now, if you want to be a useful, happy Christian, just get to work and do not go to sleep. We have enough sleepy Christians. If a church has nothing for you to do, do not go into it. Find some church where you can find something to do. If you want to be a healthy Christian, you have got to work. Joseph's captivity was turned when he began to work for others.

⬦ ⬦ ⬦ ⬦ ⬦ ⬦ ⬦ ⬦ ⬦ ⬦ ⬦ ⬦ ⬦ ⬦ ⬦ ⬦

THE CHURCH IS THE BRIDE OF CHRIST—LET US SEEK TO JOIN A CHURCH AND WORK TO GLORIFY GOD.

*L*AY *M*INISTRY

When I was in Edinburgh, they told me that one of the worst places was in Cow Court, one of the darkest streets of Edinburgh. But, rain or shine, Sundays and cloudy days, every night right along for twenty-nine years, there has been a religious meeting there. One man took it on Monday, and another on Tuesday, and another on Wednesday, and so on through the week.

I like the Scotch grit; there's no cessation in the meetings. Just at a quarter to eight a man came and backed himself up against a lamppost. In a few minutes he had a crowd; and then they marched up to the building—it was a miserable-looking building. I had the pleasure of trying to get the people of Edinburgh to put him up a good building, but without this they have had a meeting right along every Sunday for between thirty and forty years.

Some of the finest men today in Scotland who are standing for the Son of God were converted at Cow Gate near to that lamppost. There are many of these laymen, not only willing to go there nights, but at other times. And so it can be today if the Christian men and women will rise up and say, "I'll not wait any longer for any Christian committee to put me to work!"

BE FAITHFUL WHERE THE LORD HAS PLANTED YOU AND GO AND PREACH TO YOUR NEIGHBORS.

*D*ECEPTION OF *S*ATAN

*H*ow many men all over the world are being deceived by the god of this world? It has been asserted that during the late Franco-German war, German drummers and trumpeters used to give the French beats and calls in order to deceive their enemies. The command to "halt" or "cease firing" was often given by the Germans, it has been said, and the French soldiers were thus placed in positions where they could be shot down like cattle.

Satan is the archenemy of our souls, and he has often blinded our reason and deceived our conscience by his falsehoods. He has often come as an angel of light, concealing his hideousness under a borrowed cloak. He says to a young man, "Sow your wild oats. Time enough to be religious when you grow old."

The young man yields himself to a life of extravagance and excess, under the false hope that he will obtain solid satisfaction, and it is well if he awakens to the deception before his appetites become tyrants, dragging him down into depths of want and woe.

Satan promises great things to his victims in the indulgence of their lusts, but they never realize the promises. The promised pleasure turns out to be pain, the promised heaven a hell.

SATAN—THE DECEIVER OF THE BRETHREN.

THE CONFESSION OF SIN

Go downtown and you will see in every window the announcement, "This is the cheapest store in town," and that you can buy goods cheaper there than anywhere else. It is very singular that you can buy them cheapest at every store, and they say, "That is the very lowest, and we cannot get them any less."

It seems to me there is a good deal of lying in business transactions, and we need a revival of honesty. Then the world will have confidence in their Christianity. Straighten out all these differences. If a man has defrauded another man, go and make restitution and people will have confidence in your piety. But to come here and pray and sing, and try to cover up these things by loud singing and praying, is not going to deceive the Almighty.

You may deceive your neighbor, you may deceive yourselves, but you can't deceive God.

GOD KNOWS THE THOUGHTS AND
INTENTIONS OF THE HEART, EVEN
IF WE HAVE DECEIVED OURSELVES.

THE VALUE OF TESTIMONY

*F*aith is a belief in testimony. It is not a leap in the dark, as some tell us. That would be no faith at all. God does not ask any man to believe without giving him something to believe. You might as well ask a man to see without eyes, to hear without ears, and to walk without feet—as to bid him believe without giving him something to believe.

When I started for California I procured a guidebook. This told me, that after leaving the state of Illinois, I should cross the Mississippi, and then the Missouri, get into Nebraska, then go over the Rocky Mountains to the Mormon settlement at Salt Lake City, and proceed by the way of the Sierra Nevada into San Francisco. I found the guidebook all right as I went along; and I should have been a miserable skeptic if, having proved it to be correct three-fourths of the way, I had said that I would not believe it for the remainder of the journey.

❖━━━━━━━━━━━━━━━━━❖

JESUS SAID, "I AM TRUTH." WHY
SHOULDN'T WE FULLY BELIEVE HIM?

A Description of the Trinity

It is not long ago, it just seems the other day, when my dear friend Dr. Matheison, now in heaven, told me he was preaching the gospel in Scotland, and a minister told him he had in his congregation a little retarded boy. He did not know what to do with him. He had spoken to him many times, but the boy always said, "Ye must wait till I come to you, and when I come I'll sing ye a song and tell ye a story; but ye must wait till I come to ye."

The minister heard that the boy was dying, and he went to him and said, "Sandy, you promised me that you would sing me a song and tell me a story before you died. Will you tell it now?"

"Yes, minister," replied the boy. "Three in one and one in three, and Jesus Christ, He died for me, and that's it."

I tell you, I would rather be a little retarded boy and know that, than be one of the mightiest and so-called wisest men in the city of Chicago, and not believe that Jesus took my place and died for me on Calvary's cross. The gospel is very simple. It is very easy to understand.

EVEN THE LITTLE CHILDREN
UNDERSTOOD JESUS.
THE GOSPEL IS EASY TO UNDERSTAND.

THE NATURE OF TRUST

A prominent and much loved minister died, one of those ministers who had had a large salary and had given it all to the poor where he lived. He was a public man struck down in the prime of his life. As he lay on his dying bed, he thought of leaving his wife and children unprovided for, and there came a cloud over his mind. He was greatly depressed. He couldn't get above it.

While he lay there, thinking of the sad lot of his loved ones, a little bird with a worm in its mouth lit on his windowsill. With that a warmness came into his heart, and the thought came into his mouth, "If God can take care of that bird, He can take care of my wife and children." At once the trust of a child came into his heart and the burden rolled away. He knew he could trust his family to God.

As they bore him away, the whole city was moved. The rich and the poor were there, and for miles up to the cemetery the streets were lined with people weeping. This poor man was hardly laid away in his grave before a friend rose and proposed that £5000 Sterling ($25,000) be raised for the widow and her children, and it was done. God took care of the trusting minister's widow and orphans.

BLESSED IS THE MAN
WHO TRUSTS IN THE LORD.

THE WORK OF WITNESSING

Winning souls to God is a work that anyone can do. A little girl only eleven years old came to me in a Sunday school and said, "Won't you please pray that God will make me a winner of souls?" I felt so proud of her, and my pride was justified, for she has become one of the best winners of souls in this country. Suppose she lives sixty years and goes on winning four or five souls every year. At the end of her journey there will be three hundred souls on the way to glory. And how long will it be before that little company swells to a great army?

Don't you see how that little mountain stream keeps swelling till it carries everything before it? Little trickling streams have run into it, till now, a mighty river, it has great cities on its banks, and the commerce of nations floating on its waters.

So when a single soul is won to Christ you cannot see the result. A single one multiplies to a thousand, and that into ten thousand. Perhaps a million shall be the fruit, we cannot tell. We only know that the Christian who has turned so many to righteousness shall indeed shine forever and ever.

Look at those poor fishermen, Jesus' disciples, how unlettered. They were not learned men, but they were great in winning souls. Any Christian can work for God.

"HE THAT WINNETH SOULS IS WISE"

Salvation of a Drunken Woman

A lady came into the office of the New York City Mission, and said that, although she did not think she could do very much of active work for the Lord, she should like to distribute a few tracts. One day she saw a policeman taking a poor drunken woman to jail—a miserable object, ragged, dirty, with hair disordered. This lady's heart went out in sympathy toward her.

She found the woman after she came out of jail and just went and folded her arms around her, and kissed her. The woman exclaimed, "My God! What did you do that for?" She replied, "I don't know, but I think Jesus sent me to do it."

The woman said, "Oh, don't kiss me anymore; you'll break my heart. Why, nobody has kissed me since my mother died." But that kiss brought the woman to the feet of the Savior, and for the last three years she has been living a godly Christian life, won to God by a kiss.

LISTEN AND OBEY, FOR THERE
IS TRULY NO OTHER WAY.

THE POWER OF SMALL THINGS

When H. M. Stanley was pressing his way through the forests of darkest Africa, the most formidable foes that he encountered, those who caused most loss of life to his caravan and came the nearest to entirely defeating his expedition, were the little Wambutti dwarfs. So annoying were they that very slow progress could be made through their dwelling places.

These little men had only little bows and little arrows that looked like children's playthings, but upon these tiny arrows there was a small drop of poison which would kill an elephant or a man as quickly and as surely as a Winchester rifle. Their defense was by means of poison and traps. They would steal through the darkness of the forest and, waiting in ambush, let fly their deadly arrows before they could be discovered. They dug ditches and carefully covered them over with leaves. They fixed spikes in the ground and tipped them with the most deadly poison, and then covered them. Into these ditches and on these spikes man and beast would fall or step to their death.

You may think that your sins are little things, but they are tipped with deadly poison. Sin is a deadly trap that destroys all who fall into it.

SIN IS AS DEADLY AS POISON.

*L*AW V. *G*RACE

I pity those who are always hanging around Sinai, hoping to get life from the law. I have an old friend in Chicago who is always lingering at Sinai. He is a very good man, but I think he will have a different story to tell when he gets home to heaven. He thinks I preach free grace too much, and I must confess I do like to speak of the free grace of God.

This friend of mine feels as though he has a kind of mission to follow me and whenever he gets a chance he comes in with the thunders of Sinai. The last time I was in Chicago, I said to him, "Are you still lingering around Sinai?"

"Yes," said he, "I believe in the law."

I have made inquiries, and I never heard of anyone being converted under his preaching. The effects have always dwindled and died out. If the law is the door to heaven, there is no hope for any of us.

⋆◈⋆◈⋆◈⋆◈⋆◈⋆◈⋆◈⋆◈⋆◈⋆◈⋆◈⋆◈⋆

THE WONDERFUL GIFT OF THE FREE GRACE OF GOD.

CONFESSION OF CHRIST

When I was in Ireland I heard of a man who got great blessings from God. He was a businessman—a land proprietor. He had a large family, and a great many men to work for him taking care of his home.

He came up to Dublin and there he found Christ. And he came boldly out and thought he would go home and confess Him. He thought that if Christ had redeemed him with His precious blood, the least he could do would be to confess Him and tell about it. So he called his family together and his servants, and with tears running down his cheeks he poured out his soul to them, and told them what Christ had done for him.

He took the Bible down from its resting place and read a few verses of gospel. Then he went down on his knees to pray, and so greatly was the little gathering blessed that four or five out of that family were convicted of sin. They forsook the ways of the world and accepted Christ and eternal life. It was like unto the household of Cornelius, which experienced the working of the Holy Spirit. And that man and his family were not afraid to follow out their profession.

WHERE TWO OR THREE ARE GATHERED
IN MY NAME, THERE AM I.

THE NATURE OF OPPORTUNITY

A sculptor once showed a visitor his studio. It was full of statues of gods. One was very curious. The face was concealed by being covered with hair, and there were wings on each foot.

"What is his name?" said the visitor.

"Opportunity," was the reply.

"Why is his face hidden?"

"Because men seldom know him when he comes to them."

"Why has he wings on his feet?"

"Because he is soon gone, and once gone can never be overtaken."

It becomes us, then, to make the most of the opportunities God has given us. It depends a good deal on ourselves what our future shall be. We can sow for a good harvest, or we can do like the Sioux Indians, who once, when the United States Commissioner of Indian Affairs sent them a supply of grain for sowing, ate it up. Men are constantly sacrificing their eternal future to the passing enjoyment of the present moment; they fail or neglect to recognize the dependence of the future upon the present.

MAY WE NOT FAIL TO SEE
THE DEPENDENCE OF THE FUTURE
ON THE PRESENT DECISIONS.

AN EXAMPLE OF THANKFULNESS

I remember a man who was a carpenter, who used to belong to the same church that I did. He always wore a smile—not a forced smile, but a natural one. Every time he got up in prayer meeting a smile passed over the whole congregation. A smile was on his face before he said anything, and he always began by saying, "Bless the Lord!" It wasn't one of those insincere expressions that we hear sometimes, it was honest and hearty.

While at work one day he cut his thumb so that it only held by a little piece of skin. I said to myself, the next time I see that man he probably won't smile or say, "Bless the Lord!" But at the next weekly prayer meeting he was there, and the first thing he said was, "Bless the Lord! I cut my thumb, but I didn't cut it clear off!"

Most of us would have changed our shout into a wail, and it would have been a doleful sort of testimony. I would as soon get a blast of chilly east wind in March, right off the Maine seacoast, as to meet some of those Christians who are not thankful. Let us be cheerful, and bright, and sincere. If God has been good to us, let us give thanks.

LET US GIVE SINCERE THANKS,
FOR GOD HAS TRULY BLESSED US.

THE DANGER OF TEMPTATION

I remember when I was a young Christian I used to think that it would be easier after a time, and that when I had been a Christian fifteen or twenty years, I should have but few temptations and difficulties. But I find that the longer I live the more dangers I see surrounding me.

Why, Samson judged Israel for twenty years and then fell into sin; and how many men there are who fall in their old age. I don't mean that they are finally lost, but they fall into sin. They make some mistake, or their old temper springs up, and they do some mean thing, and very often the church has not as much sympathy with such persons as it ought to have.

Too much is frequently expected of new Christians. There is a great difference between a person falling into sin and loving sin. If you fall into sin and all the time hate it, go and tell God all about it, for He is faithful and just to forgive us our sins and to cleanse us from all unrighteousness.

IF WE CONFESS OUR SINS, HE IS
FAITHFUL AND JUST AND WILL
FORGIVE US OF ALL UNRIGHTEOUSNESS.

THE NEED OF A SEARCHING HEART

Listen to the confession of a minister, sensible of his tendency to neglect spiritual things, and especially of the difficulty of this duty: "I have lived," said he, "more than forty years and carried my heart in my bosom all this while, and yet my heart and I are as great strangers and as utterly unacquainted as if we had never come near one another. Nay, I know not my heart, I have neglected my heart."

We are fallen into an Athenian age, spending our time in nothing more than in telling or hearing news. How go things here? How there? How in one place? How in another?

But who is there that is inquisitive concerning the inner life: How are things with my poor heart? Oh, the days, months, years, I bestow upon sin, vanity, the affairs of this world, while I afford not a minute to converse with my own heart concerning its need.

GUARD YOUR HEART, FOR
IT IS THE WELLSPRING OF LIFE.

HEAVEN'S PEOPLE

I remember after being away from home some time, I went back to see my honored mother, and I thought in going back I would take her by surprise and steal in unexpectedly upon her. But when I found she had gone away, the old place didn't seem like home at all. I went into one room and then into another, and I went all through the house, but I could not find that loved mother, and I said to some member of the family, "Where is Mother?" and they said she had gone away.

Well, home had lost its charm for me. It was that mother who made home so sweet to me, and it is the loved ones who make home so sweet to everyone. It is the loved ones who are going to make heaven so sweet to all of us. Christ is there; God the Father is there; and many, many who were dear to us who lived on earth are there—and we shall be with them by and by.

HOME SWEET HOME, WHERE
OUR HEARTS LONG TO REST FINALLY.

THE VITAL NATURE OF PRAYER

Dr. Guthrie thus speaks of prayer and its necessity, "The first true sign of spiritual life, prayer, is also the means of maintaining it. Man can as well live physically without breathing, as spiritually without praying. There is a class of animals—the cetaceans, neither fish nor seafowl—that inhabit the ocean. It is their home, they never leave it for the shore. Yet, though swimming beneath its waves and sounding its darkest depths, they must regularly rise to the surface that they may breathe the air. Without that, they could not exist in the dense element in which they live, and move, and have their being.

"And something like what is imposed on them by a physical necessity, Christians have to live by a spiritual one. It is by regularly ascending up to God, by rising through prayer into a loftier, purer region for supplies of divine grace, that we maintain our spiritual life. Prevent these animals from rising to the surface, and they die for want of breath. Prevent the Christian from rising to God, and he dies for want of prayer. 'Give me children,' cried Rachel, 'or else I die.' 'Let me breathe,' says a man gasping, 'or else I die.' 'Let me pray,' says the Christian, 'or else I die.'"

IT IS BY REGULAR ASCENDING TO GOD
THROUGH PRAYER THAT WE MAINTAIN
A HEALTHY SPIRITUAL LIFE.

THE RESURRECTION BODY

Take a little black flower seed and sow it; after it has been planted some time, dig it up. If it is whole you know that it has no life; but if it has begun to decay, you know that life and fruitfulness will follow. There will be a resurrected life, and out of that little black seed will come a beautiful, fragrant flower.

Here is a disgusting grub, crawling along the ground. By and by old age overtakes it, and it begins to spin its own shroud, to make its own sepulchre, and it lies as if in death. Look again, and it has shuffled off its shroud, it has burst its sepulchre open, and it comes forth a beautiful butterfly, with different form and habits.

So with our bodies. They die, but God will give us glorified bodies in their stead. This is the law of the new creation as well as of the old: light after darkness, life after death, fruitfulness and glory after corruption and decay.

"I AM THE RESURRECTION, AND THE LIFE"

GOD'S LOVE FOR SINNERS

*A*nother young man told me last night that he was too great a sinner to be saved. Why, they are the very men Christ came after. The only charge they could bring against Christ down here was that He was receiving bad people. They are the very kind of people He is still willing to receive. All you have to do is to prove that you are a sinner, and I will prove that you have got a Savior. And the greater the sinner, the greater need you have of a Savior. You say your heart is hard? Well, then, of course you want Christ to soften it. You cannot do it yourself. The harder your heart, the more need you have of Christ. The blacker you are [in sin], the more need you have of a Savior.

If your sins rise up before you like a dark mountain, bear in mind that the blood of Jesus Christ cleanses from all sin. There is no sin so big, or so black, or so corrupt and vile, but the blood of Christ can wash it away.

•◦•··•◦•··•◦•··•◦•··•◦•··•◦•··•◦•··•◦•··•◦•··•◦•·

WHAT CAN WASH AWAY MY SINS,
NOTHING BUT THE BLOOD OF JESUS.
WHAT CAN MAKE ME WHOLE AGAIN,
NOTHING BUT THE BLOOD OF JESUS.

Additional copies of this book are available
from your local bookstore.